Mont Blanc
5 Routes to the Summit

*For Marius, Arian, Athina,
and Joséphine...
...and to the day that we will
climb up there together.*

Through his work as a mountain guide, François Damilano has shared his passion for high places with clients on innumerable climbs in the Alps and the Himalayas. His love of writing and photography has led him to write a number of books on mountaineering ("Chemins de Gel", with Bernard Amy and Gérard Kosicki; "Montagne Passion" with Claude Gardien).

In conjunction with Godefroy Perroux, he has also edited a series of mountaineering guidebooks for the Mont Blanc Massif and a collection of ice-climbing guides.

He is a technical advisor for several mountain equipment manufacturers (Petzl, Millet, Adidas Eyewear) and plays an active role in the development and testing of tomorrow's mountaineering equipment.

Mont Blanc

5 Routes to the Summit

The Goûter Route
Mont Blanc "ordinary route"
The Three Monts Route
The Grands Mulets Route
The Pope Route
The Miage - Bionnassay Route

François **Damilano**

JMEditions

Miage - Bionnassay - Mont Blanc: one of the great alpine traverses

Foreword

Keys to a successful climb

Mont Blanc is famous, it doesn't need any publicity.
The beauty of the mountain and the prestige of reaching the highest point in Western Europe are enough to attract several thousand budding ascensionists every year.

With so many people – of all levels of ability – aspiring to reach the summit, it is important to point out that climbing Mont Blanc is neither insurmountably difficult nor a simple ramble in the hills.

"Mont Blanc - 5 Routes to the Summit" describes the five most classic routes to the "Roof of Europe". The highly detailed route descriptions unveil the individual complexities and characters of each itinerary, providing all the information needed for a successful and enjoyable climb.

To maximise the enjoyment and minimise the risks...
To ensure the reality is even better than the dream...

With help from:

Commandant de Bonneville
Haute-Savoie "Peloton de Gendarmerie de Haute-Montagne"

Yannick Giezendanner
Meteorologist – Météo France

Jean-Pierre Herry
Médical Doctor at ENSA (National Ski and Mountaineering School)

Luc Moreau
PhD in alpine geography and glacier specialist

Thanks to:

Jean Annequin - Françoise Aubert - Fabrizio Bertinetti - Christine Bottollier - Arnaud Boudet - Bibliothèque de Chamonix - Bibliothèque de l'ENSA - Xavier Chappaz - Catherine Claude - Mario Colonel - Pierre Curral - Monica Dalmasso - Raoul Damilano - Christophe Devouassoux - Sabina Di Fatta - Béa Dumond - Jean-Luc Favre - Anne Gery - Pierre-André Gobet - Noëlle Grobel - Antoine Haincourt - Didier Josèphe - Patrick Le Brazidel - Fred Lorenzio - Cécile Masson - Guillaume Menozzi - OHM Chamonix - Michel Paccalet - Dek Palmer - Bruno Pelissier - Pierre Pizzano - David Ravanel - Laurence Ravanel - Marie et Jean Rouxel - Tony Ryan - Arnaud Sage - Yvonne Sibbald - Marie-Hélène Simond - René Simond - Jean-René Talopp - Bridget Temple - Pascal Tournaire - Murielle Tuaz - Patricia Tuveri - Jean-Luc Vanacker - Jean-Louis Verdier.

Photo credits

Collection Damilano except Philippe Batoux: p. 8 - Mario Colonel: inside front cover; p. 40; p. 46; p. 65; p. 68; p. 118; p. 148 - Pierre Gignoux: p. 87 - Pierre-André Gobet: p. 86; p. 87 - Jean-Pierre Herry: p. 18 - Yves Lambert: p. 48; p. 49; p. 50; p. 60 - Florence Lelong: p. 53 - Luc Moreau: p. 22 - Françoise Rouxel: p. 76; p. 82 - Pascal Tournaire: p. 2; p. 12; p. 17; p. 25; p. 30; p. 53; p 97; p. 103; p. 104; p.124, p. 126; p. 137; p. 138; p. 139; p. 140; p. 141; p. 142; p. 156; p. 157; p. 158; back cover - rights reserved - X.

Cover: First Mont Blanc...

Warning

Mountaineering is a dangerous sport that should only be undertaken by those with a full understanding of the risks involved and the training and experience to evaluate them. Users of this guidebook do so at their own risk. The authors cannot be held responsible for accidents that may occur on any of the routes described in this book.

How to use this guide

✔ The guidebook introduction includes general information about Mont Blanc and advice on the best way to prepare for your climb.

✔ Each route is illustrated by a sketch map and a photograph that shows the general line of ascent, which will help you situate the route geographically and visualise what the terrain is like.

✔ The stated climbing times are valid for parties of equal ability, with good climbing conditions. They assume that the climbers are correctly acclimatised and that they have sufficient technical ability not to find the route unduly difficult. There are many factors that can lead to these times being increased. The times do not take into account breaks.

✔ Each route is described and illustrated step-by-step, from the start point in the valley to the summit.

✔ Most of the photographs were taken looking in the direction of travel. However, in order to give more precise information, some photos were taken from other points of view and will need to be interpreted with care.

✔ Each route is described as a round-trip, i.e., using the same route for the descent as for the climb. Of course, any climb can be combined with any descent, in which case the description of the descent route must be taken from the relevant chapter.

✔ Where necessary, the most interesting variations to the standard route have been described.

✔ These variants are indicated by a number accompanied by the letter "a".

✔ In the text, all place names have been left in French (e.g. Mont Blanc) unless there is an accepted English translation (e.g. Refuge du Gouter = Gouter hut). However, on the sketch maps and diagrams, the French names have been used, as these are the names you will find on topographical maps and signposts etc.

✔ A guidebook is a source of information; it is no substitute for experience or personal initiative.

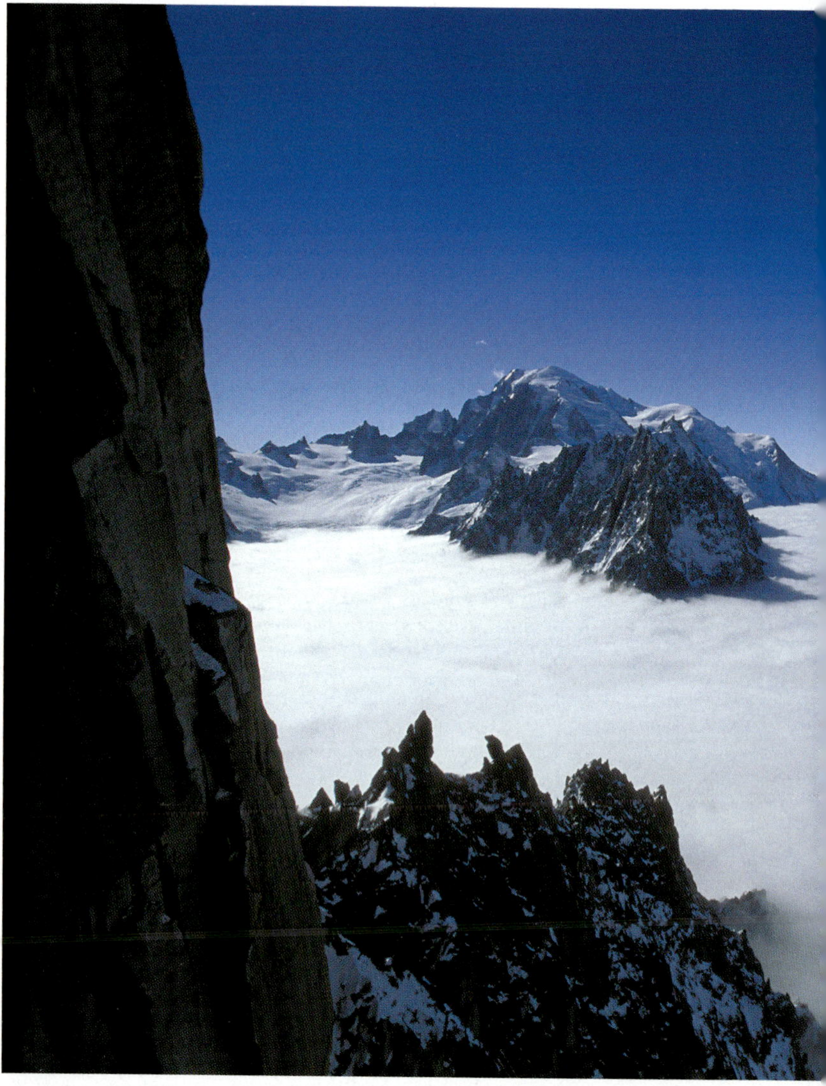

Altitude 4808

Slip from dream to reality.

Imagine the world of altitude and prepare yourself.

Remember the adventures of the pioneers and follow their tracks.

Climbing Mont Blanc is true mountaineering!

Before going any further, two dangerous misconceptions need to be laid to rest.
"Climbing Mont Blanc is easy!"
Wrong. An ascent of Mont Blanc may not involve acrobatic climbing techniques, but it is a long climb at high altitude that should not be undertaken lightly.
"Mont Blanc is just a walk!"
Wrong. There is no easy path to the top. Going up snow slopes or across crevassed glaciers in crampons, and climbing narrow ridges or towers of broken rock would not fall into most people's definitions of "just a walk".

You may not need to be a top-class mountaineer to climb Mont Blanc, but it is much more than just another hike. Which is part of the attraction.

There are a few common sense rules that must be followed:
- The high mountains are an unforgiving place. To enjoy this world in safety requires a certain amount of knowledge and experience.
- Mont Blanc is not the place for learning the rudiments of mountaineering.
- Mont Blanc should not be a first high mountain summit!

Newcomers to mountaineering who wish to climb Mont Blanc should not be offended if their guide first suggests a day on a glacier (to learn how to walk in crampons), an "easy" summit (physical and mental preparation), and a "preliminary 4000m summit" (to evaluate your own abilities, acclimatisation). This type of preparation will greatly increase your chances of reaching the top and enjoying the climb.

Last, but by no means least, it is important to keep in mind the idea that when you have reached the summit you have only done half the route. You then have to get down, and the descent can feel extremely long when for your body is already tired from the climb.

The Aiguille du Midi and the four 4000m: Mont Blanc du Tacul - Mont Maudit - Mont Blanc - Dôme du Goûter

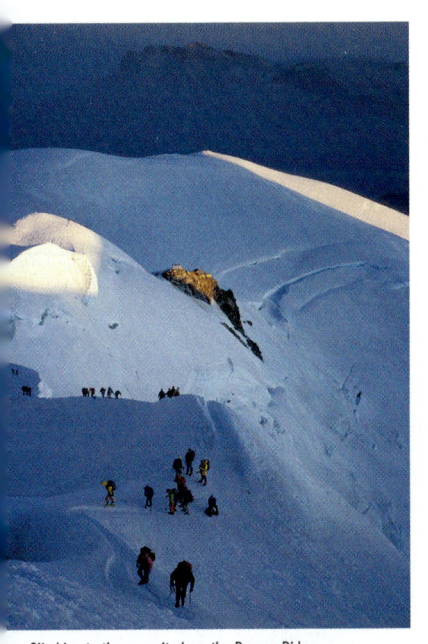

Climbing to the summit along the Bosses Ridge

> "Mont-Blanc and the Valley of Chamonix, and the Mer de Glace, and all the wonders of that most wonderful place are above and beyond one's wildest expectation. I cannot imagine anything in nature more stupendous or sublime. If I were to write about it now, I should quite rave – such prodigious impressions are rampant within me…"
>
> **Charles Dickens - 1846**

Is Mont Blanc over-crowded?

Mont Blanc is a unique mountain for symbolic and for aesthetic reasons. It is the highest point in Europe - many geographers consider Mount Elbrus (5633m), in the Caucases, to be outside Europe. It is also a very distinctive peak, not just the highest point in an amorphous mass of poorly delineated summits.

It is very high: just under 5000 metres is not an insignificant altitude.

It is accessible: despite its imposing shape, there are routes to the top that are within the capabilities of most climbers, even the least experienced.

This is a heady mixture that attracts large numbers of climbers during the summer season and leads to two recurring problems:

- Certain routes, especially the Goûter Route, become over-crowded at peak times, which can lead to safety problems. It can also pose problems at some of the huts.
- Mont Blanc attracts a certain number of would-be ascensionists who have little or no experience of the mountains. They are unaware of what such a climb involves and therefore poorly prepared for what they will be up against.

Reasons for taking a guide

- Statistics show that only about a third of "unguided" parties reach the summit of Mont Blanc.
- There is no such thing as zero risk, even when climbing with a mountain guide, but guides have the technical skills and knowledge of the mountain environment to reduce the risks to a minimum.
- A guide's advice in preparing for the climb will help you develop your skills and sustain your motivation.
- A guide has the experience needed to choose the best route according to the conditions to be found on the mountain.
- A guide will share every step of the climb with his/her climbing partners, helping to calm fears and shouldering the responsibility for finding the best way to overcome the difficulties encountered and for setting a suitable pace.
- A guide will not be over-awed by the difficulty of the route, nor by the importance of the undertaking: he/she will provide a balanced assessment of any situation that you may encounter.

Where to find a guide?

Many mountain guides belong to what are called "Compagnies" in order to share organisational facilities (office, reception services, reservations, brochures). The first "Compagnie" to be formed was in Chamonix, in 1821. The Courmayeur "Compagnie" was formed in 1885, followed by St. Gervais in 1864. All of the major Alpine and Pyrenean Valleys now have their own "Compagnies" and half of France's 1500 mountain guides belong to a "Compagnie".

The remaining 750 mountain guides are "independent". They work alone, in small groups or through agencies. The Yellow Pages for mountain areas have a mountain guides section (guides de haute montagne) and there are a great many Internet sites advertising guiding services.

When to climb Mont Blanc

There is no hard and fast rule, but the most favourable period, in terms of prevailing weather conditions, tends to be from June to September. The ski-touring season for Mont Blanc, via the Grands Mulets Route, starts in March.

In the mountains, weather conditions can be much more extreme than at lower altitudes. Above a certain altitude, almost all precipitation falls as snow or hail. Even in the middle of summer, a period of bad weather can make climbing impossible and the mountain may not "come into condition" for several days after the weather improves.

There are days when all the surrounding summits are baking under clear blues skies, but Mont Blanc is blanketed by a characteristic lenticular cloud, known as "the donkey" (l'âne). Under these conditions, a blizzard may be raging around the summit, with violent winds that make any upward progress impossible. Even on "good weather" days, a strong northerly wind can bar access to the summit ridges.

It is often extremely cold; even when it is +30°C in Chamonix or Saint-Gervais, it may be -20°C at the top of Mont Blanc.

The combined effects of the wind and the low temperature (the wind-chill factor) turns the summit into a veritable North Pole!

When the summer is dry, with long periods of good weather, freeze-thaw action turns the summit snowfields into sheets of ice, making it much harder to get a good grip with your crampons. Under such conditions, certain sections of the route become technically more difficult and more delicate to negotiate. The glaciers become "crevasse fields" (Mont Blanc du Tacul, Grands Mulets, Glacier du Dôme) and complicated to cross. During heat waves or droughts (summer 2003), the entire mountain starts "moving", increasing the frequency and size of stone falls (Aiguille du Goûter).

The definition of good conditions or bad conditions is highly subjective. Judgements are linked to the experience, technical ability and fitness of the mountaineer; in the mountains, it is better to refrain from making definitive statements and peremptory remarks when it comes to the difficulty of a route or climbing conditions.

10 TIPS BEFORE SETTING OUT

1 - Choose your route to suit the conditions on the mountain.
2 - Choose a route that is within your technical and physical abilities.
3 - Study guidebooks and maps.
4 - Learn how to navigate and how to use navigational aids.
5 - Check the weather forecast.
6 - Be well equipped.
7 - Learn the techniques you will need, get fit and get acclimatised.
8 - Don't blindly follow other people's tracks. Learn to trust your own judgement.
9 - Stay clear headed.
10 - Come back in one piece!

Weather

Yan Giezendanner, forecaster and mountain weather expert, explains what is meant by "bad weather".

Cold and wind at the Col de la Brenva

The wind

The wind has two effects. First, it has a mechanical effect, upsetting a climber's balance. Second, it amplifies the sensation of cold. 0°C with a 60km/hr wind feels like -15°C under still conditions, and -20°C with a 60km/hr wind feels like -35°C. Once the wind speed exceeds 70km/hr it is usually impossible to reach the summit.

However, depending on the direction from which it is blowing, the wind does not affect all of the routes in the same way.

- Northerly winds (north-west through

Lenticular cloud overflowing onto Mont Blanc du Tacul and the Aiguille du Midi

to north-east): above 60km/hr, the wind makes the routes on the north face (Three Monts, Grands Mulets, Goûter) more difficult. Routes on the south face will be sheltered from the wind, except for the final section just below the summit. At the same time,

clouds may back up against the north face whilst the south face remains clear.
- Southerly winds (south-east through to south-west): even gentle winds can produce the Foehn Effect: damp air (clouds, snow) builds up on the Italian (south) side and overflows onto the French (north) side. These clouds may just cover the summit, but they may also descend as low as the Grands Mulets. Under such conditions, it is never certain whether you will be able to reach the summit, even if the wind is light. If the wind is strong, it will be impossible to get to the summit.

The arrival of bad weather

When the weather forecast predicts a beautiful day followed by the arrival of very bad weather within 36 hours, there would seem to be a long-enough "window" to climb Mont Blanc before the bad weather arrives. However, a meteorological phenomenon, which is innocuous elsewhere but very important for Mont Blanc, has to be taken into account. Before the weather front arrives, a characteristic lenticular cloud will gradually form over the top of the mountain. At first, a weak band of clouds will shroud the summit, followed a few hours later by a vast bank of cloud, inside which a blizzard will be blowing. This cloud will gradually cap all of the neighbouring high peaks, such as the Aiguille du Goûter and the Aiguille du Midi.
Under these strange conditions, the rest of the Alps may be bathed in sunshine while a snowstorm rages at the top of Mont Blanc. The people of Chamonix refer to this as "the donkey on Mont Blanc".
The information given by the weather forecast can be supplemented by observing how the weather in the mountains is evolving. For example, if when looking from the Goûter hut towards the Southern Alps you can see lens- or fish-shaped clouds and the wind is blowing from the south-west, a lenticular cloud will form over Mont Blanc within the next few hours. The

Arrival of a weather front over Mont Blanc and the Dôme du Goûter

Lenticular cloud capping Mont Blanc and the Dôme du Goûter

summit conditions will be very difficult, but a very early start from the hut may allow you to beat the weather.

Storms
The arrival of a storm front results in violent winds, lightning, snow, hail and extreme cold. The passage of a front usually takes several hours, although it can take up to 24 hours when the weather is coming from the south-west.
Storms can build up in two different ways: first, the "in-situ" formation of cumulonimbus clouds and second, the arrival of a storm front that moves in the same way as a standard weather front.
- "In-situ" (or local) cumulonimbus clouds can form in a matter of hours (sometimes much more quickly!), but the storm will not usually break until the middle of the afternoon. This should give you enough time to climb Mont Blanc and get back down again, but it is important to keep an eye on

how quickly the clouds are building. This type of storm is very difficult for meteorologists to predict with precision.

- On the other hand, meteorological computers allow the movement of weather fronts and associated storms to be predicted quite accurately. However, variations in the speed in which the front moves may still cause errors in the timing of the forecast.

Here too, climbers can supplement the weather forecast with their own observations:

• A rapid and constant decrease in atmospheric pressure indicates the arrival of a storm front. Your altimeter-barometer must be read and adjusted regularly.

• A regular increase in wind speed accompanied by the arrival of high clouds marks the approach of a storm.

• The sky clouds over quickly. Fluffy clouds forming at high altitude and lenticular or tower-shaped clouds dotting the horizon are precursors of a change in the weather.

• The inexorable approach of a band of black cloud or a front sparkling with lightning should be seen as the signal to beat a retreat.

Météo France
Météo Haute-Savoie :
+33(0)8 36 68 02 74
3615 meteo
www.meteo.fr

Preparation and medical advice

Interview with Dr Jean-Pierre Herry, doctor at ENSA (National Ski and Mountaineering School)

Do you have to be a top-class athlete to climb Mont Blanc?

No, most people are capable of climbing Mont Blanc as long as they have done a certain amount of fitness training.

Getting to the top is often a question of stamina. Training should be based around long periods of moderately intense exercise, such as jogging, walking or cycling.

No matter how fit you are, it is essential to acclimatise to the altitude.

Given good weather conditions, any healthy person who does a reasonable amount of regular exercise should be able to climb Mont Blanc.

What does "being acclimatised" mean?

Acclimatisation is a very important factor in reaching the top. In the mountains, the altitude, or more precisely the resulting hypoxia – a lack of oxygen due to the fall in atmospheric pressure – reduces the body's physical capacities.

The body compensates for this lack of oxygen by:

- increasing the breathing and heart rates (adaptation phenomena during the first hours and days at high altitude),
- increasing the number of red blood cells to increase the blood's ability to transport oxygen (acclimatisation that occurs after six to eight days at altitude).

During the week prior to climbing Mont Blanc, acclimatisation is best achieved by doing a number of other climbs, at higher and higher altitudes, and spending nights in mountain huts.

What sort of medical conditions would prevent someone from going to altitude?

At moderate altitude (2500m) there are very few contra-indications (chronic breathing difficulties, non-stabilised heart conditions).

However, you have to be in excellent health to withstand the harsh climatic conditions found at high altitude.

If you are suffering from a medical condition, whether it be temporary or permanent, that reduces the body's resistance you should think twice about trying to climb Mont Blanc. Such conditions include:

- metabolic illnesses (e.g. insulin-resistant diabetes),
- pregnancy (first or last three months),
- acute fevers, convalescence from an illness, etc,

Climbing Mont Blanc is not advisable for children below the age of 16.

NUTRITION IN THE MOUNTAINS

Before the climb

Absorb as much carbohydrate (pasta, rice, etc) as you can the evening before the climb. The storage of glycogen is more efficient in the recovery phase after exercise.
Eat light before the strenuous effort of the climb itself.
In practical terms: in huts, dinner is served between 6 p.m. and 7.30 p.m., breakfast at 2 a.m.

During the climb

Top up your energy levels by eating 50g of simple sugars (sweet foods) every two hours.

For example, 50g of glucose corresponds to 66g of raisins or 7 dry figs or 10 sweets. Take one litre of tea or herbal tea sweetened with ten sugars per litre. In reality, lack of appetite and/or the cold will stop you from assimilating all of this food.

After the climb

Drink a lot of sweetened drinks as soon as you stop.
Eat a lot of carbohydrates (pasta, rice, etc) during the evening meal.
Drink a lot.

What sort of drink to take?

When climbing Mont Blanc, it is impossible to avoid a certain degree of dehydration: dry air, lack of drinks. It is important to limit water loss due to sweating by wearing the right clothing and moving at the right speed. You need to drink small quantities regularly. One litre of sweetened drink should be enough for the climb.

This information is given as a guideline only.
It is also important to take snack foods that you like eating.
When the effects of altitude are combined with tiredness, it is much easier, and much more comforting, to eat something you like.

What are the risks of climbing Mont Blanc without being acclimatised?

The greatest risk is severe altitude sickness. It can set in when you spend a few hours above 3000 metres and is characterised by headaches, loss of appetite, nausea, abnormal tiredness and insomnia. These symptoms are often blamed on the hut environment (the uncomfortable conditions) or tiredness from the climb, but they are also the effects that hypoxia has on the body. However, not everybody reacts to altitude sickness in the same way.

Some people suffer at altitudes as low as 2000m and may need to descend quickly if the symptoms become serious. Tests to measure one's susceptibility to altitude sickness can be carried out at specialist mountain medicine centres.

What should I do if I feel the symptoms coming on?

Altitude sickness regresses with acclimatisation and disappears when you lose height.

Spurred on by the desire to get to the top, it is sometimes difficult to decide to turn round, even when suffering from the discomfort of the symptoms. The decision about whether to continue or to turn back should be based on a number of factors, including the distance you are from the summit, whether you feel capable of getting to the top and the weather conditions.

Are there other risks?

Although a lack of stamina and insufficient acclimatisation are the major risks involved in climbing Mont Blanc, the effects of the cold and of the sun should not be forgotten.

When the wind is strong, especially on the summit ridge, cases of frostbite to the face are quite common. This type of frostbite is not as serious as frostbite to the feet or hands, but you may not be aware it is happening. Every bit of skin must be protected. Superficial frostbite to the cornea, which is caused by strong side winds and leads to blurred vision, can be prevented by wearing ski goggles.

FIRST AID KIT

- Bandages.
- Protection to stop blisters or "hot spots" forming (elastoplast).
- Blister treatment (Urgo/Compeed).
- Sun cream and lip cream.
- Aspirin.
- Eye lotion.
- Anti-diarrhoea.
- Diamox is very effective in preventing altitude sickness, but it has unpleasant side effects (diuretic effect, pins and needles in hands and feet).
  It is available on prescription only.

Mountain medicine consultations:
Avicenne Hospital - Bobigny
Tel: + 33 (0)1 48 95 58 32
Cochin Hospital - Paris
Tel: + 33 (0)1 58 41 16 80
Hôpital Sud - Grenoble
Tel: + 33 (0)4 76 76 54 94
Briançon Hospital
Tel: + 33 (0)4 92 20 10 33

ENSA medical service
Tel: + 33 (0)4 50 55 30 07

Internet sites:
www.ensa.jeunesse-sports.fr/medical
www.ffme.fr/medical

Another danger is that of sunburn. The effects of solar radiation, especially UV radiation, are much more intense at high altitude and when you are on snow. UV radiation is not filtered by the atmosphere when you are at high altitude.

It is essential to wear category IV sunglasses with side pieces.

The skin and lips must be protected with high protection factor sun cream (at least SPF 30), applied every two hours.

What is the age limit for climbing Mont Blanc?

Many youngsters from Chamonix, accompanied by an experienced adult, have climbed Mont Blanc. By choosing the best possible conditions, they have been able to "run" to the top in one day and have therefore avoided being affected by altitude sickness. However, a young person who climbs Mont Blanc in the traditional way, with a night in a hut, will be much more susceptible to the effects of altitude. They will also have less certain weather conditions. Don't forget that children generally prefer to play in physical and climatic conditions that are very different to those found in the high mountains.

If they are fit and have a reasonable amount of stamina, there is no reason why older people shouldn't climb Mont Blanc, but they will need more time to reach the summit.

Glaciology

Altitude measured by GPS on 5 September 2003: 4808,45m

**Three questions for ...
Luc Moreau,
glaciologist.**

How thick is the ice at the top of Mont Blanc?

In 1891, an engineer called Imfeld dug a 15m-deep tunnel into the top of Mont Blanc to try and find rock on which to anchor Jules César Janssen's astronomical observatory. He failed. The observatory was just "placed" on the summit and mounted on jacks so it could be raised as snow built up around it (precipitation, which falls as snow, is the equivalent of about one metre of water per year). Despite these precautions, the flow of the cold glacial mass (-15°C) caused the observatory to "drift" until it was buried by falling snow. The wooden turret, which continued to protrude above the surface, was dismantled and taken to the Alpine Museum in Chamonix, where it is still on display. The dismantling of this building provided Joseph Vallot with wood for heating the observatory he built on the rocks that emerge at the foot of the Bosses Ridge.

In June 1983, the glaciology laboratory drilled a 16m-deep borehole into the ice without reaching rock. At the moment we have no accurate measurement of the thickness of the ice, but it is thought that it could be as much as 30 or 40 metres.

Does this summit ice "move"?

All the world's glaciers move, by deformation and flow for cold glaciers, and also by sliding for temperate glaciers that are not frozen to the bedrock. Crevasses are often seen at the summit of Mont Blanc. Sometimes they are perpendicular to the axis of the ridge (Vallot, 1890) and sometimes they show the radial movement of the ice mass (crevasse summer 2003, SE of the summit, showing movement towards the Brenva Glacier). The snow that falls on the northern summit feeds the famous Bossons Glacier, which descends to an altitude of 1300m, a record for the Alps. Its flow rate is very high, around 200 metres per year!

Studies of the Bossons Glacier, in the earliest days of glaciology, helped people understand that glaciers flow from the top, where they form, towards the bottom, where they melt.

Lastly, what is the exact height of Mont Blanc?

The summit has been covered in ice for about three million years. Its "whaleback" shape is a result of the action of the wind on the covering of ice. On a century-by-century timescale, the variations in the shape and thickness of this ice are small, so the height of Mont Blanc is quite stable. The last measurement, taken on 5th September 2003, produced a height of **4808,45 metres**, two metres lower than the height measured in 2001.

The Mont Blanc and the Bossons Glacier

Gear

Personal
- 40-litre rucksack
- Mountaineering boots – warm and suitable for crampons
- Gaiters (with a strap under the boot)
- Crampons with anti-balling system
- Classic ice axe
- 1 or 2 telescopic ski poles
- Lightweight and comfortable climbing harness + cow's-tail with screw-gate karabiner
- Descender or Reverso-type belay device
- Head torch with new batteries
- Lightweight helmet (especially for the Aiguille du Goûter)
- Warm socks (+ spare pair)
- Carline-type themal T-shirt, avoid using cotton as it absorbs moisture and dries slowly
- Polar fleece sweater
- Down or Thermolite jacket
- Carline-type or stretch polar fleece leggings
- Waterproof jacket (with hood) and over-trousers (Gore Tex)
- Hat or headband
- Balaclava
- Scarf
- Sunglasses
- Ski goggles
- Pair of lightweight gloves
- Pair of warm gloves or mittens
- Mini-wash kit: hand-wipes, moisturising and high SPF sun creams
- Mini-first aid kit: Compeed, Elastoplast, aspirin or paracetamol, eyewash (see p.20)
- 1-litre insulated water bottle
- Snack food
- Pocket knife
- Optional: a lightweight sheet sleeping bag for the night in the hut

For each party
- 50m (minimum) single rope
- 2 x 60cm slings
- 2 x 120cm slings
- 6 karabiners
- 2 screw-gate karabiners
- 4 ice screws
- Self-rescue/hauling equipment (prussik loops, self-jamming pulley)
- Mobile phone
- Navigation equipment: compass + altimeter + 1/25,000 IGN map
- 1 survival blanket
- Rubbish bag

Huts provide crockery and cutlery, meals and blankets for the bunks.
There is no need to take these things with you.

Huts

The route descriptions in this guide mention three types of accommodation:

- **Huts** (Cosmiques, Grands Mulets, Tête Rousse, Goûter, Tré-la-Tête, Conscrits, Plan Glacier, Durier, Gonella). Huts have a communal refectory and dormitories with mattresses and blankets. During the summer, these huts are staffed and provide drinks and meals. They are supplied by helicopter. There is usually no running water. Reservation is obligatory, as a matter of safety, and reservations should be confirmed three days before going up (based on the weather forecast).

The Goûter hut is usually over-booked, so it is necessary to reserve well in advance (by the beginning of June). Otherwise, you can telephone at the last minute to see if there has been a cancellation. If you can't respect your booking, please telephone the warden – it is a matter of courtesy and may allow someone else to take your place.

- Winter room
This is the part of the hut that is always open, even when the hut isn't staffed. It usually consists of a dormitory with mattresses and blankets, plus a cooking area with a few utensils.

- Shelter (Vallot)
Shelters are small and very basic bivouac huts, generally for use in emergencies. The Vallot shelter has a rescue beacon.

Inside the Durier Hut

Altitude 4808

Tête Rousse hut
+33 (0)6 19 02 90 71
Staffed from mid-June to mid-September
74 places

Goûter hut
+33 (0)4 50 54 40 93
Staffed from mid-June to mid-September
100 places

Cosmiques hut
+33 (0)4 50 54 40 16
Staffed from 15th February to 15th October
145 places

Plan de l'Aiguille hut
+33 (0)6 65 64 27 53
Staffed from 15th June to 15th September
40 places

Grands Mulets hut
+33 (0)4 50 53 16 98
Staffed from late March to late September
68 places

✓ **The right attitude at every altitude**
As part of a programme to clean up and enhance the image of its natural beauty spots, Saint-Gervais Council has launched an environmental awareness campaign. Fourteen information points will be set-up, in order to:
- reduce the chronic overcrowding of the Goûter Route to the summit of Mont Blanc,
- remind climbers that the reservation of places in huts is obligatory,
- remind climbers of the rules concerning camping rough (forbidden in protected areas),
- explain the problems caused by bivouacking around the Goûter hut,
- raise awareness of Saint-Gervais' "Pure Mountain" environmental improvement campaign.
For more information go to **www.st-gervais.net**

Altitude 4808 — 27

Tré-la-Tête hut
+33 (0)4 50 47 01 68
Staffed at Easter, Pentecost and from June to September
80 places

Conscrits hut
+33 (0)4 79 89 09 03
Staffed from mid-March to late September
94 places

Plan Glacier hut
+33 (0)4 50 93 23 25
Staffed at Ascension, Pentecost and from June to September
25 places

Durier hut
+33 (0)6 89 53 25 10
Staffed from late June to beginning of September
15 places

Gonella hut
+39 0165 885 101
Staffed from June to September
42 places

HUT DOS AND DON'TS

- It is essential to book before going up to a hut.
- Confirm three days before going up.
- Let the warden know if you can't respect your booking.
- Most high altitude huts don't have running water.
- Take your rubbish down with you.
- Fold your blankets before leaving the dormitory.
- Do not disturb people who are already in bed or still sleeping: pack your rucksack outside the dormitory.

A word from the Haute-Savoie "Peloton de Gendarmerie de Haute-Montagne"

The "Roof of Europe" is a major honey-pot for climbers in the Mont Blanc Massif. It is often the only mountain climbed by mountaineers visiting the area. The attraction that this emblematic summit holds leads to certain routes becoming over-crowded and to these routes being attempted by people who do not have the necessary technical skills or fitness. For many mountaineers, it is their first taste of high altitude climbing. The climb is often attempted with out "warming up" on smaller summits, following the logic of 'if you can do more, you can do less".

As a result, the Chamonix PGHM carries out a great many rescue missions on the routes to the top of Mont Blanc. All the routes are exposed to the usual objective dangers: stone fall, the collapse of seracs, risks linked to snow conditions at the beginning of the season, the glaciated terrain and brutal changes in weather conditions. These dangers are compounded by the high altitude. Furthermore, the technical difficulty of a route can vary significantly depending on the weather. For example, on the North Face of the Tacul, there may be a well-marked track through good snow that is easy to follow. On the other hand, after a period of intense freeze-thaw, the same slope may be covered in rock-hard ice that is much harder to climb. Similarly, in "dry" conditions the Aiguille du Goûter can be considered an easy climb; it is a very different undertaking after a snowfall, or a period of rain followed by a freeze.

The cold and the altitude increase the technical difficulties described in guidebooks. Many rescue operations are launched to help mountaineers who are suffering from the cold because they didn't have appropriate clothing or the wherewithal to shelter from bad weather. It must never be forgotten that when a storm hits Mont Blanc, a human being's limits are soon reached. This is equally true for mountain rescue personnel. Being able to contact the rescue services, via a mobile telephone or a radio, does not necessarily mean that a rescue operation can be launched immediately (or even in time), as rescuers are subject to the same weather conditions as everyone else.

In short, the popularity of these routes often leads them to be underestimated by many climbers. It is essential to remember that just because a climb is technically "easy" does not mean that it is without risk. When soaking up the magnificent view of Mont Blanc from the sunny terrace of a bar, one must not lose sight of the fact that the temperature at the top may be 30° or 35°C lower than the temperature in Chamonix, and that once you have reached the top, after an intense physical effort, you have only done half the route.

Useful addresses

Tourist Offices

Chamonix Tourist Office
+33 (0)4 50 53 00 24
www.chamonix.com

Les Houches Tourist Office
+33 (0)4 50 55 50 62
www.leshouches.com

Saint-Gervais Tourist Office
+33 (0)4 50 47 76 08
www.st-gervais.net

Courmayeur Tourist Office
+ 39 0165 842 060
www.comune.courmayeur.ao.it

Office de Haute Montagne Chamonix
+33 (0)4 50 53 22 08
www.ohm-chamonix.com
- General and practical information
(guidebooks, maps, etc).
- Information about conditions in the mountains.
- PGHM reception open every afternoon in July and August.

Rescue

International number from
a mobile telephone: 112

Chamonix PGHM
+33 (0)4 50 53 16 89

Aosta Valley Mountain Rescue
+39 0165 230 253

Chamonix Hospital
+ 33 (0)4 50 53 84 00

Weather Forecast

Haute-Savoie forecast
+33 (0)8 36 68 02 74
www.meteo.fr

Public transport

SNCF railway station Saint-Gervais – Le Fayet
+33 (0)4 50 78 45 90

SNCF railway station Les Houches
+ 33 (0)4 50 55 50 07

SNCF railway station Chamonix
+33 (0)4 50 53 07 02

Chamonix Bus
+33 (0)4 50 53 05 55

Coach office at Chamonix railway station
(Chamonix<->Courmayeur)
+ 33 (0)4 50 53 01 15

Lifts

Aiguille du Midi cable car
+33 (0)4 50 53 30 80
Reservations
+33 (0)8 92 68 00 67
The Aiguille du Midi cable car only has a limited number of places. At busy times, and no matter what type of ticket you have, you will need to get a boarding card with a cabin number from the ticket office.

Les Houches – Bellevue cable car
+33 (0)4 50 54 40 32
Open from beginning of June to late September

Les Bossons chairlift
+33 (0)4 50 53 12 39

Mont Blanc tramway
+33 (0)4 50 47 51 83
Open from May to September

Route descriptions, route finding and GPS

On the Miage - Bionnassay - Mont Blanc traverse

- The **route descriptions** in this book only contain general orientation information; they do not give precise compass bearings. There is no guarantee that visibility will be good, so it is essential to be able to read a map, take bearings and use an altimeter or GPS system.
- **GPS** is a fabulous navigational tool, but only if you know how to use it properly and interpret and analyse the data it provides. Even with a GPS you have to be able to read a map and interpret the terrain over which you are travelling. It is for this reason that only a small number of GPS points are given for each route.
- The **directions** "right hand", "left hand" or "right" and "left" are relative to the direction in which you are moving.

The directions "right bank" and "left bank" refer to the true orographical banks of the stream, glacier, valley or gully.
- **Glaciers** move continuously and the snow cover varies throughout the year. The descriptions follow the most commonly used routes, but from one year to the next, and even from one day to the next, the exact line of ascent can change. A guidebook can only give a certain amount of information. The person using the guidebook must be able to interpret this information and adapt it to the actual conditions encountered.
- The **climbing times** that are given have been shown by experience to be valid for parties of equal ability, with good climbing conditions.

They assume that the climbers are correctly acclimatised and that they have sufficient technical ability not to find the route unduly difficult. The times do not take into account breaks.

IGN TOP25 n°3531 ET map
Format UTM
WGS 84 geodesic system

Goûter Route:
Nid d'Aigle:
32T E 0329 065 N 5080 736
Baraque des Rognes:
32T E 0329 795 N 5081 225
Tête Rousse hut:
32T E 0330 590 N 5080 275
Goûter hut:
32T E 0331 510 N 5080 139
Vallot shelter:
32T E 0333 185 N 5078 418
Mont Blanc:
32T E 0334 118 N 5077 668

Miage – Bionnassay Route:
Tré-la-Tête hut:
32T E 0323 938 N 5073 400
Conscrits hut:
32T E 0326 300 N 5072 814
Durier hut:
32T E 0329 963 N 5076 925
Piton des Italiens:
32T E 0331 475 N 5078 255
Vallot shelter:
32T E 0333 185 N 5078 418
Mont Blanc:
32T E 0334 118 N 5077 668

Three Monts Route:
Aiguille du Midi:
32T E 0336 034 N 5082 725
Cosmiques hut:
32T E 0335 873 N 5082 102
Col du Mont Maudit:
32T E 0334 888 N 5079 450
Petits Rochers Rouges:
32T E 0334 283 N 5078 075
Mont Blanc:
32T E 0334 118 N 5077 668

Pope Route:
Start of Aiguilles Grises path:
32T E 0331 125 N 5075 690
Gonella hut:
32T E 0331 615 N 5076 255
Piton des Italiens:
32T E 0331 475 N 5078 255
Vallot shelter:
32T E 0333 185 N 5078 418
Mont Blanc:
32T E 0334 118 N 5077 668

Grands Mulets Route:
Plan de l'Aiguille:
32T E 0335 914 N 5085 288
Les Glaciers station:
32T E 0333 955 N 5081 438
Grands Mulets hut:
32T E 0335 053 N 5083 782
Mont Blanc:
32T E 0334 118 N 5077 668

GPS is merely an extra tool to be used in conjunction with the basic navigational trilogy of 1/25,000 scale map, compass and altimeter.
The GPS points quoted here are for reference points: huts, cable car stations, characteristic summits.
GPS is accurate to +/- 15m. The precision of the points taken from the map is, at best, +/- 25m. Conclusion: the accuracy of the point given by the GPS is +/- 40m. This margin of error must be taken into account when navigating.

32 Altitude 4808

The Five

- SALLANCHES
- CLUSES
- GENEVE

LE FAYET — Gare T.M.B.

ST-GERVAIS-LES-BAINS

LES HOUCHES — Téléphérique de Bellevue

Gare de Bellevue

Baraque des Rognes

Le Nid d'Aigle

Refuge du Go... 3817

Refuge de Tête Rousse 3167 m

Dôme du G... 4304 m

Aiguille de Bionnassay 4052 m

LES CONTAMINES-MONTJOIE

le Cugnon

Refuge Durier 3369 m

Refuge Gonella 3071 m

Aiguille de la Bérangère 3425 m

Refuge de Tré-la-Tête 1970 m

Refuge des Conscrits 2602 m

Routes

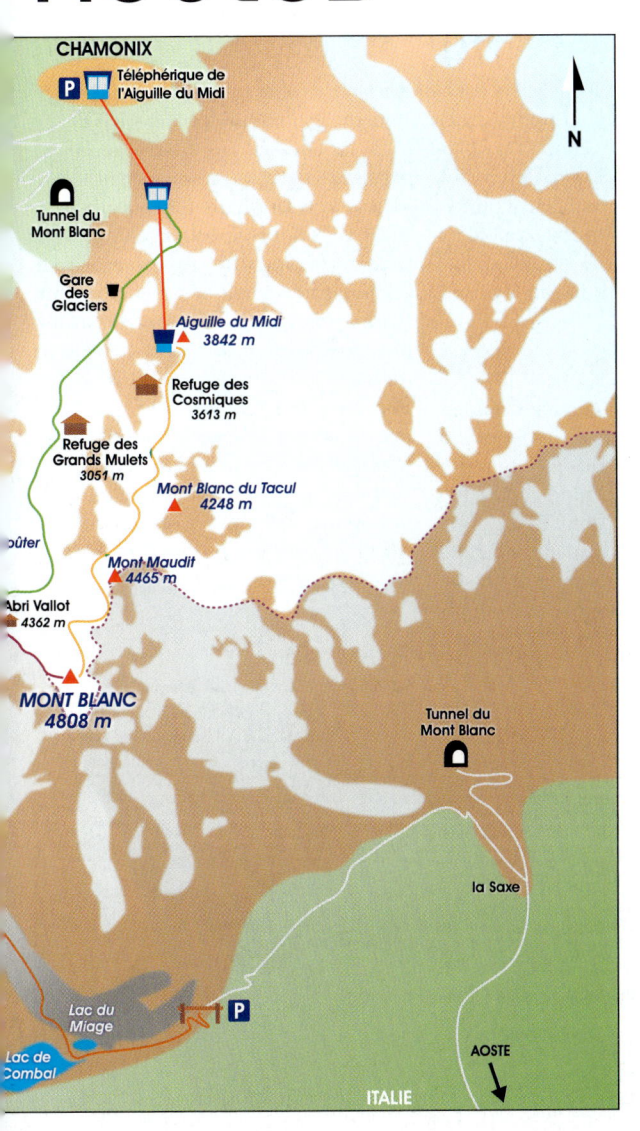

Altitude 4808 | 33

CHAMONIX

Téléphérique de l'Aiguille du Midi

Tunnel du Mont Blanc

Gare des Glaciers

Aiguille du Midi
3842 m

Refuge des Cosmiques
3613 m

Refuge des Grands Mulets
3051 m

Mont Blanc du Tacul
4248 m

Goûter

Mont Maudit
4465 m

Abri Vallot
4362 m

MONT BLANC
4808 m

Tunnel du Mont Blanc

la Saxe

Lac du Miage

Lac de Combal

AOSTE

ITALIE

N

— Goûter Route

— Three Monts Route

— Grands Mulets Route

— Pope Route

— Miage-Bionnassay Route

Mont Blanc in 10 dates

1741

William Windham and Richard Pococke, two Englishmen staying in Geneva, "discovered" the "Mer de Glace". The following year, Pierre Martel from Geneva followed in their footsteps. Their writings, which focused more on the exploits of the "explorers" than the summits climbed, caused quite a stir in the salons of Europe.

1760

The Geneva naturalist Horace Bénédict de Saussure made his first visit to Chamonix and immediately offered a reward to whoever found a feasible route to the top of Mont Blanc. As a scientist, he wanted to make detailed observations of the mountain, but he had to wait 25 years before making his own successful ascent (the third).

Another "Genevois", Marc Théodore Bourrit, also fell under the spell of the high mountains. His first visit to the Alps was such an aesthetic and intellectual revelation that he decided to dedicate all his creative energies to their portrayal. He too unceasingly encouraged attempts to climb Mont Blanc: *"To date, it is believed that no-one has achieved this feat; one is amazed that everything possible has not been tried to do this!"* He took part in several attempts himself, despite not being a natural mountaineer. His writings, in which he described both his own travels and those of others, played a large part in building Chamonix's reputation.

The Mer de Glace as seen by Marc Théodore Bourrit

1762

Pierre Simond, from Chamonix, made two exploratory journeys towards Mont Blanc, one from Montenvers via the Mer de Glace and the Glacier du Tacul, and the other via the Bossons Glacier.

1774

Pierre Simond continued his explorations. With Saussure and Jean-Laurent Jordanay, he attempted to go around to the south of the mountain and go up the Val Veny and the Glacier du Miage.

1775

On 14th July, Jean-Nicolas Couterand (son of Chamonix's inn-keeper), with François Paccard (exiled from Savoie for having acted as a guide for the bandit Mandrin), Michel Paccard and Victor Tissay reached the Grand Plateau, thereby inaugurating the route via the Montagne de la Côte and the Jonction. Considering the very real dangers involved in such an enterprise, this was a remarkable expedition. At the time, people knew very little about travelling over highly crevassed terrain and of the effects of altitude on the human body. In the autumn, Michel Gabriel Paccard (a young man from Chamonix who was studying medicine in Turin) and Thomas Blaikie (the famous Scottish gardener) also made an attempt starting from the Montagne de la Côte.

Crossing a crevasse at the Grands Mulets. W. Pitschner

1783

Despite Saussure and Bourrit's unflagging encouragement, eight years went by before the next serious attempt. Chamonix was becoming more and more popular with tourists, tourists who enthusiastically urged their guides to take up the challenge of climbing Mont Blanc.

Jean-Marie Couttet (who became one of Saussure's guides after the death of Pierre Simond) Jean-Baptiste Lombard-Meunier (nicknamed Grand Jorasse because of his imposing stature) and Joseph Carrier (known as Bouquet) decided to try again. To make the best of the available daylight, they started out from a bivouac at the top of the Montagne de la Côte. The idea of spending a night on a glacier was not yet conceivable and all previous attempts had been made from the valley with the intention of being back down before nightfall. On this occasion, the three explorers were defeated by intense heat and burning sun as they climbed the "Valley of Snow".

Worried that the guides would be discouraged by this new failure, Bourrit rushed from Geneva. Together with Paccard, he organised another expedition for 15th September. According to his report, they got close to the summit, *"I was forced to beat a retreat just as I thought my goal was within reach."* In reality, they turned round almost as soon as they reached the Jonction, beaten by bad weather and torrential rain.

With all of these failed attempts the route via Les Bossons began to look impossible and would-be ascensionists began to concentrate their energies on the Saint-Gervais side of the mountain.

1784

Paccard made several attempts throughout the summer. On 5th June, with Pierre Balmat, he once again tried to climb the Glacier du Tacul.

On the 20th, he reconnoitred the Aiguille du Goûter. During this time, Bourrit was gathering information from all possible sources. He learned that two hunters from the hamlet of La Gruaz were boasting that they had reached the summit of the Aiguille du Goûter. He talked to them, and they confirmed that the slopes above the Aiguille were not very steep.

On 10th September, accompanied by Jean-Baptiste Jacquet, Paccard once again tried to climb the Aiguille du Goûter.

On 16th September, the guides Grand Jorasse and Jean-Marie Couttet, together with the two hunters from La Gruaz, Bourrit, his dog (!), and Maxime, a farm-worker from Sallanches (nicknamed the Baron de Pierre Ronde) started out from the village of Bionnassay. The party walked all night to get to the top of the Désert de Pierre Ronde.

They had barely reached the foot of the Aiguille du Goûter when the effects of tiredness and the cold started to make themselves felt. The little group started to slow and could not keep up with the two guides who were making the pace. Maxime and Bourrit's dog, who were freezing, turned back, followed a little later by Bourrit.

In truth, Couttet and Cuidet (one of the two hunters) were worried that Bourrit and his acolytes would hold them back, so they purposely forged ahead of the rest, determined to succeed for themselves.

They climbed the Aiguille du Goûter, traversed the Dôme and almost reached the Col du Dôme.

At last an encouraging attempt; they had reached a point only 400m below the summit!

Journey of M. de Saussure to the summit of Mont Blanc. Marquardt Wocher.

1785

The winter was hard and the summer cold and wet. The weather did not settle until September. Couttet made another attempt via the Aiguille du Goûter, accompanied by the young Balmat. A hailstorm forced them to descend.

A little later, despite the bad weather that regularly plastered the high peaks with snow, Saussure made another attempt, this time in the company of the Bourrits, father and son. There were a total of 16 people in the caravan that walked up to Pierre Ronde on 13th September. On the 14th, after three hours of hard work battling against fresh snow on the ridge up the Aiguille du Goûter, the guides gave up.

1786

The question on everyone's lips was which of the two routes, the one from Saint-Gervais via the Aiguille du Goûter or the one from Chamonix via the Bossons Glacier, would give the greatest chance of success of reaching the top of Mont Blanc? On 8th June, Pierre Balmat and Jean-Marie Couttet made an attempt via the Aiguille du Goûter, after having spent the night at Pierre Ronde. The same day, Jean-Michel Tournier, François Paccard and Joseph Carrier climbed the Bossons Glacier, after having slept at the Montagne de la Côte. The Bossons party were the first to get to the Col du Dôme. When the two parties met up, they decided to continue the reconnaissance towards the Bosses Ridge. Worried that he would miss out on the first ascent, Jacques Balmat, despite not being invited, insisted on joining the Chamonix group.

"Saussure inspired that ascent, Paccard conceived it and did it, Balmat accompanied him and made it possible. It would be an injustice to deprive any of them of the merit they deserve. Let us take a brief look at two individuals who, despite having such different origins and such different natures, were united by a common destiny and saw part of Europe stretched out below their feet. What counts is the summit of life, much more than all the summits on earth."

Georges Sonnier
La montagne et l'homme - 1977

When the others went down, Balmat got left behind and was forced to bivouac near the Grand Plateau, alone and without equipment, at a height of more than 4000 metres.

8th August: First ascent of Mont Blanc by Michel-Gabriel Paccard and Jacques Balmat.

1787

3rd August: At long last, Horace Bénédict de Saussure reached the top of Mont Blanc. It is the third ascent.

Reaching the summit. MacGregor

MILLET

MOUNTAIN BY EXPERIENCE

50 ANS D'EXPERIENCE ALPINE | 50 YEARS OF MOUNTAINEERING EXPERIENCE

L'engagement de soi, la verticalité, la liberté et la technicité sont nos valeurs essentielles. Nos équipements sont conçus et réalisés en collaboration avec les conseillers techniques les plus prestigieux. Ils sont le résultat de plus de 50 ans d'expérience et destinés à affronter les conditions les plus rigoureuses. Millet, Mountain by experience.

Total personal commitment, verticality, freedom and technique, are our essential values. Our equipment is designed and made in close co-operation with the most renowned technical advisors. The result of over 50 years of experience, designed to face the most rigorous conditions. Millet - Mountains of Experience.

more infos www.millet.fr

VÊTEMENTS TECHNIQUES SACS À DOS CHAUSSURES CHAUSSONS & CORDES
TECHNICAL WEAR BACKPACKS BOOTS ROCKSHOES ROPES

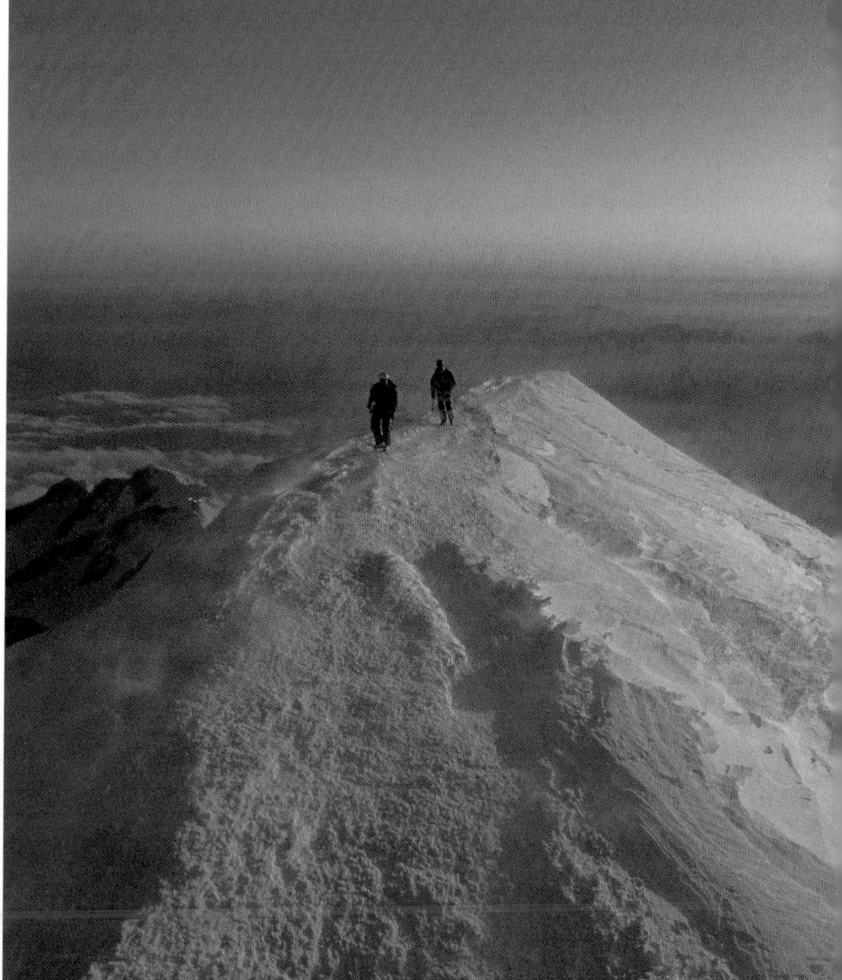

The Goûter Route

Mont Blanc's "Ordinary Route"

The Goûter Route has become the "ordinary route" for climbing Mont Blanc.
From a technical mountaineering point of view, it is the least difficult route...

... but it shouldn't be under-estimated. The climb to the Goûter hut is not a simple stroll along a path, the climb to the summit is over glaciated terrain and you have to cope with the altitude. In the middle of the summer the large number of climbers on this route also increases the objective dangers: stone fall, queues at the narrowest part of the Bosses Ridge, crowding in the hut (!). Fortunately, these irritants do not make the route any less interesting: the "Roof of Europe" is a beautiful mountain and to climb it, even by the ordinary route, is still a magnificent experience. The climb up the Aiguille du Goûter by head-torch, the slow ascent of the Dôme, followed by the narrow Bosses Ridge, lit up by the morning sun, forge indelible images in the minds of all those who venture to these heights.

CHARACTERISTICS OF THE ROUTE

ADVANTAGES
- "Only" 990m of height gain on the second day, from the Goûter hut to the summit. This is the shortest summit day for any of the classic routes on Mont Blanc.
- It is possible to divide the ascent into three stages: Day 1: to the Tête Rousse hut (3167m), Day 2: to the Goûter hut (3817 m), Day 3: to the summit.
- The difficulties increase with height, with the Bosses Ridge providing the most difficult climbing.
- Technically, it is the easiest route.
- The Bosses Ridge is very aesthetic.
- It is the route by which the greatest number of people reaches the summit.

DISADVANTAGES
- Very popular during the summer.
- Objective dangers on the Aiguille du Goûter (stone fall).
- A night in the Goûter hut can be relatively uncomfortable.
- It can be unpleasant spending a night at almost 4000m.
- The objective dangers are masked by the apparent ease of the route.
- The Bosses Ridge is steep in places and it can be icy. The entire ridge is quite airy and exposed (steep slopes on either side).
- It is the route by which the greatest number of people reaches the summit!

A little history

On 4th September 1784, during an exploratory visit to the Saint-Gervais side of Mont Blanc by Michel Gabriel Paccard, Jean-Baptiste Jacquet and Henri Pornet, Paccard and Jacquet reached an altitude of 3675m on the Aiguille du Goûter. Thirteen days later, during an exploratory visit with Théodore Bourrit, Jean-Marie Couttet and François Guidet recorded the first known ascent of the Aiguille du Goûter. They continued their reconnaissance to just past the Col du Dôme. The "Saint-Gervais Route" was born.

The best route for getting to the Dôme du Goûter, which was considered the first step in reaching the top of Mont Blanc, became a subject of intense debate.

On 8th June 1786, two parties met at the Col du Dôme. They had both set out the day before, one from the Chamonix side, the other from the Saint-Gervais side. The climbers who had come up via the Bossons Glacier and the Grands Mulets had to wait for two hours before the Aiguille du Goûter party arrived. This was taken to prove the supremacy of the "Valley of the Snows" route. The two groups joined forces to explore the Bosses Ridge, but they were quickly defeated by the difficulty of the route.

Worried that the summit would be conquered without him, Jacques Balmat had attached himself to the party from Chamonix... without being asked! When the time came to go down, he insisted on trying the Bosses Ridge one more time. When he gave up, he found that his companions had not waited for him and were already quite low down on the glacier. Did he try again to find another route? He later claimed that it was at this moment that he found the passage. There are different versions of the story

The Aiguille du Goûter, the Dôme du Goûter and the Mont Blanc

The Goûter Route

Michel-Gabriel Paccard

explaining how Balmat found himself alone near the Grand Plateau, at more than 4000m, when night fell. Charles Durier continues the story in a book he published in 1877. *"His preparations didn't take long; he put his leather bag on the ground and sat on it. He didn't even have a blanket to wrap himself in and he had nothing left to eat. (...) Towards the middle of the night, the weather worsened; it started to snow, covering him in fine needles that got inside his clothes. He used his handkerchief to protect his face and started to stamp his feet and clap his hands. As soon as he stopped, overcome by weariness, he started to succumb to a lethal drowsiness, his head fell heavily onto his chest and his eyes started to close. Every time he felt his eyes closing, he sprang awake knowing that if he fell asleep, he would never wake up. To keep his spirits up, he repeated to himself, "at least I have found the way to the top of Mont Blanc, and when Mr. de Saussure asks me to, I will take him up there!"*

The following morning, Balmat got back down to Chamonix. He had survived a bivouac on a glacier at high altitude, without suitable equipment! This involuntary demonstration shattered an ancestral fear and gave Balmat a definite psychological advantage over his competitors.

Jacques Balmat

On 6th August 1873, Leslie Stephen and the painter Gabriel Loppé climbed Mont Blanc so they would be at the summit at sunset.

"And suddenly began a more startling phenomenon. A vast cone, with its apex pointing away from us, seemed to be suddenly cut out from the world beneath; night was within its borders and the twilight still all around; the blue mists were quenched where it fell, and for the instant we could scarcely tell what was the origin of this strange appearance. Some unexpected change seemed to have taken place in the programme; as though a great fold in the curtain had suddenly given way, and dropped on to part of the scenery. Of course a moment's reflection explained the meaning of this uncanny intruder; it was the giant shadow of Mont Blanc, testifying to his supremacy over all meaner eminences."

Sir Leslie Stephen - The Playground of Europe

The Goûter Route — 45

The Bionnassay Glacier as seen from the Pavillon de Bellevue. Jean-François d'Ostervald – 1826

The Goûter Route

Route description

Mont Blanc
Refuge du Goûter
Refuge de Tête Rousse
Nid d'Aigle

Route tips

By taking one of the first trams of the day to the Nid d'Aigle you will be able to climb up to the Tête Rousse hut in the cool of the morning and stop off for an unhurried lunch. You will then arrive at the Goûter hut early enough to relax for a while before the hut fills up at the end of the afternoon.

In summer, by leaving the Goûter hut at around 2 a.m. you will have the whole day ahead of you to climb to the summit, at a reasonable pace, and be back down early enough to catch a tram back to the valley.

Setting off by torchlight makes the rather monotonous climb to the Dôme du Goûter much more interesting and means that you will have the first light of dawn to spur you on along the Bosses Ridge. Arriving at the summit in the pure dawn light, as Mont Blanc casts its shadow over the lands to the west, is a magical experience.

The Goûter Route

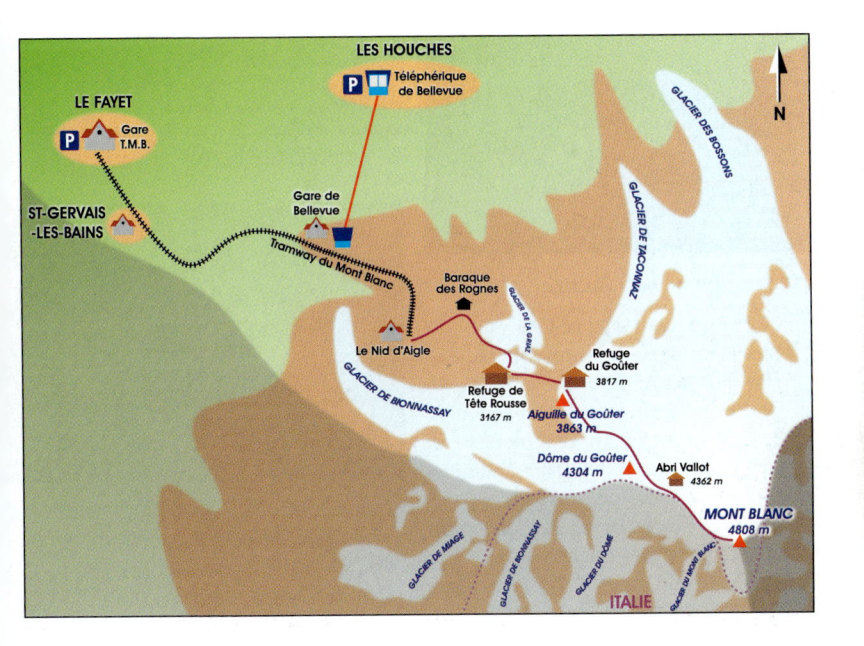

Day 1 = 5 hours (+1445m)

- Nid d'Aigle (2372m) -> Baraque des Rognes (2768m) = 1hr (+396m)
- Baraque des Rognes (2768m) -> Tête Rousse hut (3167m) = 1hr 30mins (+399m)
- Tête Rousse hut (3167m) -> Goûter hut (3817m) = 2hrs 30mins (+650m)

Day 2 = 10 hours 30 minutes (+996m/-2436m)

- Goûter hut (3817m) -> Shoulder below Dôme du Goûter (4260m) = 2hrs (+443m)
- Shoulder below Dôme du Goûter (4260m) -> Col du Dôme (4255m) = 15mins (-5m)
- Col du Dôme (4255m) -> Vallot shelter (4362m) = 30mins (+107m)
- Vallot shelter (4362m) -> Mont Blanc (4808m) = 2hrs (+446m)
- Mont Blanc (4808m) -> Nid d'Aigle (2372m) = 5hrs (-2436m)

GPS

Nid d'Aigle:	Tête Rousse hut:	Vallot shelter:
32T E 0329 065 N 5080 736	32T E 0330 590 N 5080 275	32T E 0333 185 N 5078 418
Baraque des Rognes:	Goûter hut:	Mont Blanc:
32T E 0329 795 N 5081 225	32T E 0331 510 N 5080 139	32T E 0334 118 N 5077 668

The Goûter Route

From the Nid d'Aigle to the Tête Rousse hut

✓ At the beginning of the summer, before the TMB opens, the path to the Nid d'Aigle follows the railway line. Be careful, wind-slab avalanches are possible between the Col du Mont Lachat and the Nid d'Aigle.

① Start point, two alternatives:

- Le Fayet, TMB station (Tramway du Mont Blanc), opposite the railway station. This is the highest rack-and-pinion railway in France. It will take you up to the Nid d'Aigle, at 2372m, in about one hour. This fabulous journey takes you through all the different stages of alpine vegetation and offers magnificent views of the Mont Blanc chain. The tramway's three engines, Anne, Marie and Jeanne, were named after the daughters of the person who owned the line until 1956.

- Les Houches, Bellevue cable car station. If you are based in the Chamonix Valley, you can join the TMB tram at the little station above the Col de Bellevue by taking the Bellevue cable car from Les Houches. Be careful to check the tram timetable to ensure that there is a connection with the cable car.

② From the TMB terminus at the Nid d'Aigle, head south along the wide track. After 50 metres, take the path on the left (red marks) ignoring the paths on the right, which go up to the Bionnassay Glacier.

③ Follow the hairpins up the escarpment that overlooks the tramway station, and then go across the Désert de Pierre Ronde.

The Goûter Route

④ A well-marked path goes up the south-east flank of Les Rognes, just below the ridge, to the Baraque des Rognes (2768m, 1hr). The cabin was renovated in 2003.

⑤ From the cabin, head south-east (névés) to get to the ridge that drops down from the Aiguille du Goûter and divides the La Griaz Glacier from the Tête Rousse Glacier. Follow the obvious path up the ridge (snow in places).

⑥ Once at the top of the ridge (3100m, cairns), go across the Tête Rousse Glacier, heading slightly uphill (crampons useful), to get to the Tête Rousse hut (3167m, 1hr 30mins).
If you do not want to go to the hut, go straight up the Tête Rousse Glacier, staying just below the Payot ridge.

From the Tête Rousse hut to the Goûter hut

✓ The approach to the Goûter hut should be considered a climb in its own right. Climbers undertaking this route, the West Face of the Aiguille du Goûter, should have appropriate gear and be reasonably at ease when walking on snow or scree, and when scrambling up steeper rocks. A helmet is essential for this part of the climb. Crampons and ice axe are often necessary for crossing the Grand Couloir.

⑦ From the Tête Rousse hut, go up the left bank of the Tête Rousse Glacier. The slope gradually gets steeper and leads to a system of ledges. The path, which has some quite awkward sections, climbs a slight depression under the long ridge that separates the Tête Rousse and Bionnassay Glaciers (cables). The last platform provides a sheltered place from which to observe the stone fall activity in the Grand Couloir. Rocks regularly sweep down this snow and ice gully, falling from the Aiguille du Goûter directly onto the Bionnassay Glacier.

⑧ The Grand Couloir should be crossed extremely carefully, but as quickly as possible. Before setting off, you should judge the speed at which other climbers are moving so that you are not held up in the middle of the gully. A steel cable has been strung between the banks of the gully. It can be used as a hand-line when there is the right amount of snow in the gully; otherwise it is of no help.

✓ Unfortunately, some guidebooks suggest using the Payot Ridge or the Rochers Rouges Ridge (on the right bank of the Grand Couloir) as access routes to the Goûter hut. These routes are not to be recommended, as climbers on these ridges often knock rocks down into the Grand Couloir, making life even more dangerous for climbers following the standard route.

The Goûter Route | 51

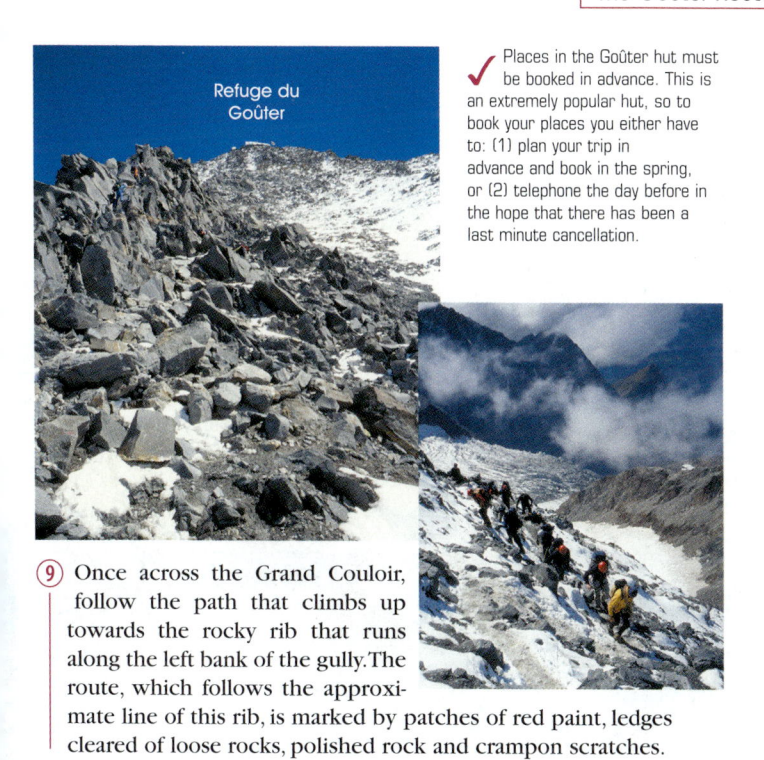

✓ Places in the Goûter hut must be booked in advance. This is an extremely popular hut, so to book your places you either have to: (1) plan your trip in advance and book in the spring, or (2) telephone the day before in the hope that there has been a last minute cancellation.

⑨ Once across the Grand Couloir, follow the path that climbs up towards the rocky rib that runs along the left bank of the gully. The route, which follows the approximate line of this rib, is marked by patches of red paint, ledges cleared of loose rocks, polished rock and crampon scratches.

⑩ Just below the hut (3817m), two sections of the path have been equipped with cables for use as hand-lines/belays. The first cable is at 3570m, the second at 3670m.

✓ At the beginning of the season, when the Aiguille du Goûter is still covered in snow, the top of the slope may be unstable: beware of wind-slab avalanches.

The Goûter Route

From the Goûter hut to the summit of Mont Blanc

✓ A little advance planning makes life a lot easier. When you get to the hut, go up a little further to check out the first part of the route. Sort out your gear (crampons and ice axe neatly stored outside the hut, boots tied together and placed on one of the shelves in the entrance-way). Keep your head-torch and toilet kit with you. Pack your sack that evening. In the morning, don't waste time at breakfast (one member of the party queues at the counter, whilst the other(s) try to save a place at a table). After breakfast, gear-up quickly. This will save you a lot of time and energy - the success of the climb also depends on sorting out these little details.

⑫ The first part of the route is almost flat. Go across the "campground", where some people will have bivouacked, either under canvas or in an igloo.

⑪ Climb above the hut to gain the snowy crest of the Aiguille du Goûter.
Head south-south-east towards the Dôme du Goûter.

⑬ The next section is easy. The route heads left (east) over two rises, both at 3845m and with a slight descent to 3840m between them (15mins).
The route trends left again to go over two more rises before reaching the foot of the wide slope that forms the north-west face of the Dôme du Goûter (15mins, 30mins from the hut).

The Goûter Route 53

⑭ Climb (south-east) the slope towards the summit of the Dôme du Goûter. If the route has been well tracked, it will zigzag up the slope to make the climb easier. There are a few crevasses, but they are usually easy to cross or go around. Towards the top of the slope, head east-south-east to contour round just below the summit of the Dôme itself. Cross the shoulder between the Pointe Bayeux (4258m) and the Dôme du Goûter (4304 m) at around 4260m, and go across to the Col du Goûter. There is a bergschrund at the break of the slope (2hrs).

✓ If the weather or the visibility are bad, it is better to turn round before the last leg leading to the Col du Dôme, as navigation becomes much more difficult after this.

⑮ Cross the gentle north-east slope of the Dôme du Goûter, descending slightly to go just below (around 4240m) and to the left of the Col du Dôme (4258m) (15mins, 2hrs 45mins from the Goûter hut).
This is a good place to have a rest – it is comfortable and much less exposed to the wind than the Bosses Ridge.

⑯ Keep heading south-east and climb the first slopes of the Bosses Ridge.
Stay right of the Vallot Observatory (scientific observatory, closed to the public) to reach the Vallot shelter (4262m, 30mins).

54 | The Goûter Route

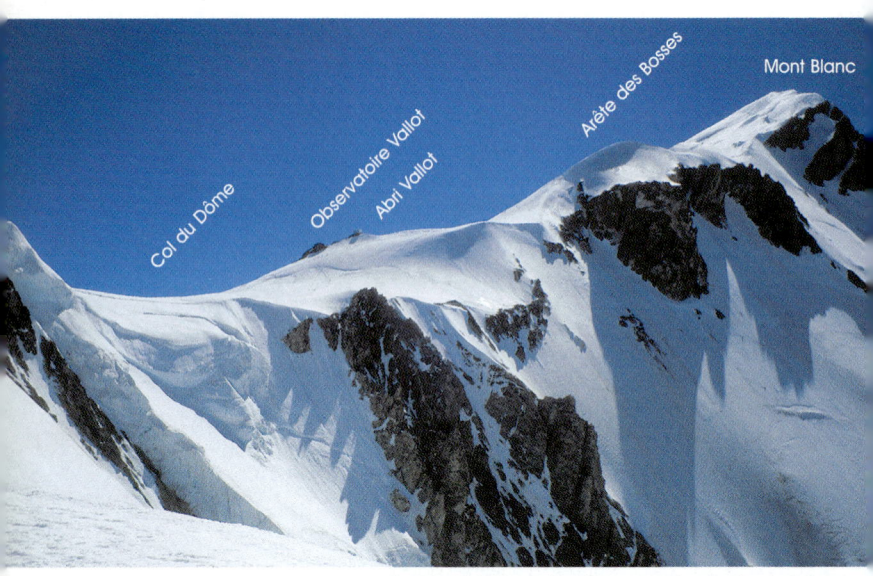

From the Col du Dôme to Mont Blanc, as seen from the Piton des Italiens

THE VALLOT SHELTER SHOULD ONLY BE USED IN EMERGENCIES.

Anchored to the Rochers Foudroyés, it was built to shelter climbers in difficulty, caught out by bad weather, or descending from the long and difficult routes on the Italian side of Mont Blanc. The hut has a radio for contacting the rescue services. This hut should in no circumstances be used as a normal mountain hut; it is not an extra stopping-off point on the ordinary route up Mont Blanc.

The limited amount of space in the hut must always be available for climbers for whom finding adequate shelter may be a matter of life and death. Furthermore, overuse by "passing climbers" leads to gradual deterioration of the hut and disgusting hygienic conditions in and around the building.

It is also a fallacy that it is possible to rest at such high altitude to recover your strength before attacking the last part of the climb. This is especially true if you are already suffering from the first symptoms of altitude sickness (excessive tiredness, sleepiness, nausea, headaches, arrythmia).

At this altitude, there is only one rule for those who are feeling ill or who have overestimated their capabilities – turn around and go down. Generally, the symptoms of altitude sickness disappear once you get back to the Goûter hut!

The Goûter Route

(17) Pass the hut on the right and cross (south-east) a small, gently sloping plateau, followed by the steep and often icy slope that leads to the base of the Bosses Ridge. You are now at the foot of the "Dromedary's Humps".

✓ Dromedary's Humps?

Why "Dromedary's Humps" ("Bosses du dromadaire") when there are two humps on the ridge and dromedaries only have one? In fact, the ridge gets its name from a comparison made by the Geneva-born writer Bourrit, who was talking about the whole mountain when he wrote: "Mont Blanc looks like a dromedary; its rump faces Geneva and the Vaud; its hump overlooks the Tarentaise on one side and Chamonix on the other and its head dips down towards the Aosta Valley and the Piedmont."

Petite Bosse   Grande Bosse

(18) Go over the Grande Bosse (4513m), and then the Petite Bosse (4547m), staying on the Italian side of the ridge – cornices often present.

(19) Climb the final sustained slope, staying to the left of the Rochers de la Tournette (4677m).

(20) Follow the magnificent summit ridge, mostly on the Italian side. The slope becomes easier angled and forms a beautiful whaleback as it reaches the summit. (2hrs, 5hrs 30mins to 6hrs from the Goûter hut).

The Goûter Route

> *"In the heavens, a few stars blink once more and then fade.*
> *Walls of ice and stone glisten at our feet. In front of us the sun, fleshy and alive, rises steadily and surely, brooking no argument. It takes possession of the space, as it creeps over nicks and peaks, cutting the walls of ice and rock from the night.*
> *We are at the top of Mont Blanc."*
>
> **Gaston Rebuffat**
> Mont Blanc, jardin féerique - 1962

The Goûter Route

DESCENT BY THE GOÛTER ROUTE

㉑ From the summit of Mont Blanc, follow the ridge, first towards the west, and then towards the north-west. At first almost flat, it soon dips down towards the Rochers de la Tournette (4677m). Pass to the right of the Rochers de la Tournette and go down the slope to the "Dromedary's Humps". Go over the Petite Bosse (4547m), and then the Grande Bosse (4513 m), staying mostly on the Italian side of the ridge. Go down the steep slope to the Vallot shelter (30mins, 4362m).

㉒ Still heading north-west, go down the sustained slope that runs out near the Col du Dôme at around 4240m. From here, it is possible to go down to the Grands Mulets Hut, via the Grand Plateau and the Petit Plateau (see Grands Mulets Route p.100). Go round to the right of the Col du Dôme (4248m) and make a gently rising traverse across the north-east slopes of the Dôme du Goûter (30mins). Go over the shoulder, at around 4260m, staying to the left of Pointe Bayeux (4258m) - bergschrund.

The Goûter Route

㉓ The slope plunges down the north-west face of the Dôme. Go down, first trending west (left) to avoid the steeper slopes below Pointe Bayeux.
Then descend the large slope towards the Aiguille du Goûter (heading north-west), some crevasses (30mins).

㉔ Go along the summit ridge of the Aiguille du Goûter, over four small rises.
Go across the "campground" plateau.
The hut is to the left, below the ridge. (3782m, 1hr 30mins to 2hrs from the summit of Mont Blanc).

㉕ The descent from the Aiguille du Goûter can be quite tricky when it is covered in snow or ice, or when the ground is wet. Furthermore, the mental and physical tiredness brought on by the climb can make it seem quite daunting and unpleasant. It is important to stay alert; a climb is only over when you are back down in the valley!

The Goûter Route 59

㉖ Below the hut, follow the cables and the marks on the rock to the traverse across the Grand Couloir, staying on the left of a rocky rib.

㉗ Traverse the gully, watching out for the frequent stone falls.
Once on the right bank of the Grand Couloir, go down an awkward path (cable, metal ladder) through a small depression.

㉘ Descend the left bank of the Tête Rousse Glacier to reach the Tête Rousse hut - easy (1hr 30mins). From the Tête Rousse hut, head north across the flat part of the glacier to reach a good path (cairns).

Réfuge de Tête Rousse

60 | The Goûter Route

㉙ Go down the path, which winds through a line of cliffs between the Tête Rousse and La Griaz Glaciers.
From the foot of the cliffs, go across a flat area of scree to the Baraque des Rognes.

㉚ The path now descends towards the south-west, staying just below the Les Rognes Ridge, and goes across the edge of the Désert de Pierre Ronde to reach the TMB station at the Nid d'Aigle (1hr).

✓ **Variant for the descent from the Tête Rousse hut.**
When there is a lot of snow, it is possible to descend the steep snow slope just below the hut towards the south-west. From the bottom of this snow slope, go across the scree on the left to get to the Bionnassay Glacier, at around 2500m, where it is flat. Follow the edge of the right bank of the glacier, moving onto the moraine when the glacier becomes chaotic. A series of paths leads back to the Nid d'Aigle (1hr).

LA MONTAGNE A L'ETAT PUR

Pour ne laisser dans la montagne que la trace de nos pas.

St Gervais
MONT-BLANC

Office de Tourisme +33 (0)4 50 47 76 08 - www.st-gervais.net

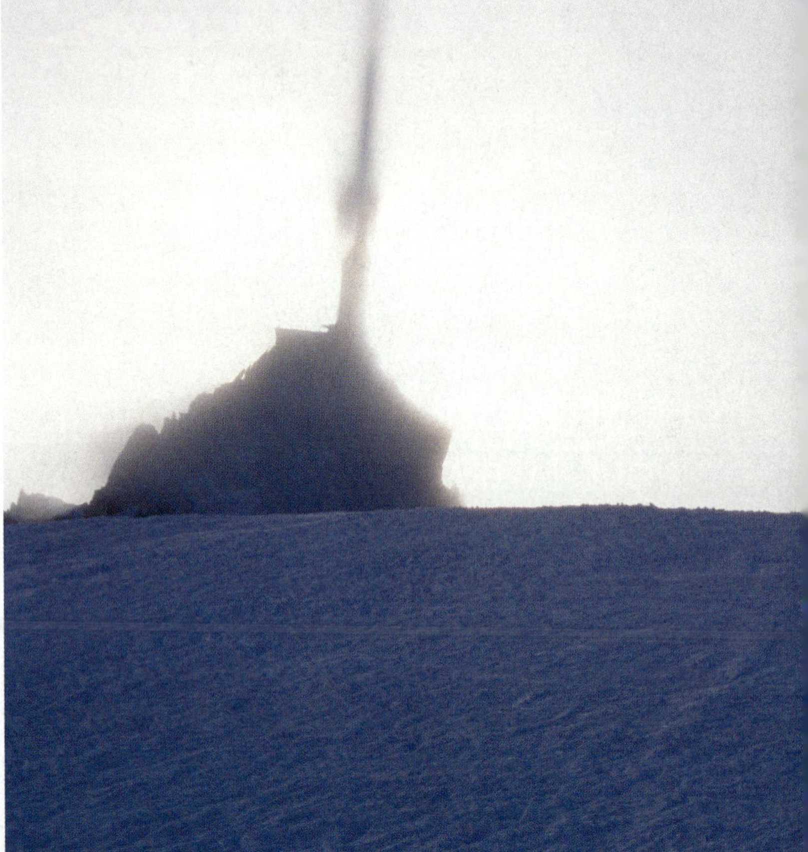

The Three Monts Route

The Aiguille
du Midi –
Mont Blanc
Traverse

The Three Monts Route

The Three Monts Route starts at the Aiguille du Midi and climbs to the summit of Mont Blanc via Mont Blanc du Tacul (4248m) and Mont Maudit (4465m).

The "Traverse of the 4000ers", which descends via the Dôme and Aiguille du Goûter is the logical continuation of this route.

With a comfortable and easily accessible (from the Aiguille du Midi cable car) hut as a starting point, it is not surprising that the "Three Monts" has become the second most popular route to the top of Mont Blanc. The continuing success of the route was assured when the new Cosmiques hut was built (in 1990) on the rocky promontory overlooking the Col du Midi. The "Three Monts" is an extremely aesthetic route that flirts with the summits of two other 4000m peaks, but it is both technically and physically much more demanding than the Goûter Route.

CHARACTERISTICS OF THE ROUTE

ADVANTAGES
- Quick and easy access to the hut from the Aiguille du Midi.
- Modern and comfortable hut.
- Possible to avoid a night at altitude by taking the first cable car in the morning (thereby limiting the effects of altitude sickness).

DISADVANTAGES
- A lot of height gain: 1425m from the Col du Midi.
- Stable snow conditions are needed for the Mont Blanc du Tacul and the Col du Mont Maudit.
- You need to move quite quickly if you want to get down to the valley the same day.
- Potential difficulties: Mont Blanc du Tacul and Mont Maudit bergschrunds, steep slopes below Mont Maudit and at the Mur de la Côte.
- No easy escape route after Mont Maudit.

A little history

The Courmayeur route

Saussure's offer of a reward, in 1760, to whoever found a feasible route to the top, immediately instigated a number of serious attempts to climb Mont Blanc. The most obvious way to the summit appeared to be via the Col du Midi, which can be reached from the Mer de Glace and the Géant Glacier, and this is the route on which the earliest attempts focused. The Mer de Glace was already well known to local guides and crystal hunters and it seemed to them, through a deceptive effect of perspective, that a rocky ridge led directly from the Col du Midi to Mont Blanc's summit icecap. None of these early explorations got any further than the seracs of the Géant Glacier.

Almost a century later, on 30th and 31st July 1855, during an expedition from Courmayeur, the Scot James Henry Ramsay, accompanied by Joseph-Marie Chabod (known as Turin) Pierre-Joseph Mochet (known as Gros) and Joseph-Marie Perrod, climbed the shoulder below Mont Blanc du Tacul, the Col du Mont Maudit, and then the Mur de la Côte. Unfortunately, by the time they got to the top of the Mur de la Côte it was too late to continue to the top of

> *"Any party that reaches the Col de la Brenva from Mont Maudit (...) must halt here, with peculiar satisfaction. Perhaps because thoughts of achievement would be scarce decent on the summit, one is presented with the opportunity of thinking them here."*
>
> **George Mallory**
> The Alpine Journal - 1918

The Aiguille du Midi, the Mont Blanc du Tacul, the Mont Maudit and the Mont Blanc

Mont Blanc, so they descended via the Corridor and the Grands Mulets. The newly formed Courmayeur Guides Company was so keen to record a successful ascent from the Aosta Valley that they wrote the ascent up as a success. They knew that the growing fashion for climbing Mont Blanc would only bring money to the valley if they had their "own" route to the top.

During the summer of 1863, they built a cabin on the rocks of the Col du Midi, to provide a half way shelter for climbers. They hoped that this would encourage further attempts, as the route from Courmayeur over the Col du Géant and past Mont Blanc du Tacul is not technically difficult, just very long.

Writing in 1877, Charles Durier noted the immediate success of the cabin. Recording the visit of two gentlemen from Geneva, he wrote, *"Seen from afar, against a backdrop of towering peaks, the little wooden building, long and narrow and with a door but no windows, looks just like a mouse trap. It is also a trap for tourists. The workers had barely regained the valley when two tourists got caught"*. The guides' strategy obviously worked! The following day, the two genlemen attempted to reach the summit only to be beaten back by violent winds.

On 13th August 1863, the first ascent of the Three Monts Route was finally completed, rather discretely, by an Englishman called Head, in the company of Julien Grange, Adolphe Orset and Joseph-Marie Perrod.

Mont Blanc and the Col du Géant. Léon Sabatier

> *"The commoners of our city (Geneva) and the surrounding area call Mont Blanc and the snow-covered mountains that surround it the Damned Mountains; and, during my childhood, I myself heard peasants say that these eternal snows were the result of a curse that the inhabitants of these Mountains had brought upon themselves by their crimes."*
>
> **Horace Benedict de Saussure**
> Voyages dans les Alpes - 1779-1796

The Three Monts Route | 67

The Top of "la côte" - T.D.H Browne

Route description

Photo labels: Mont Blanc, Mont Maudit, Mont Blanc du Tacul, Col du Midi

Route tips

Spending a night at the Cosmiques hut, one of the nicest huts in the massif, is a wonderful way in which to immerse yourself in the ambiance of the high mountains. As the sun sets over the Tacul – Maudit – Mont Blanc chain it is easy to envisage the joys of the day to come when you will be able to tread these self-same summits. An early start, at around 2 a.m., will ensure that you have enough time to reach the summit and get back down to the Nid d'Aigle in time to catch an afternoon tram back to the valley. Climbing at night, as dawn slowly breaks around you, is a magical experience.

The route can also be done in a single day, by taking the first cable car up to the Aiguille du Midi. This will allow you to delay the onset of the symptoms of altitude sickness and attack the route feeling fully refreshed after a good night's sleep in the valley. However, you will have to move very quickly if you want to get back down to the valley the same day and avoid having to spend a night in a hut during the descent.

The Three Monts Route | 69

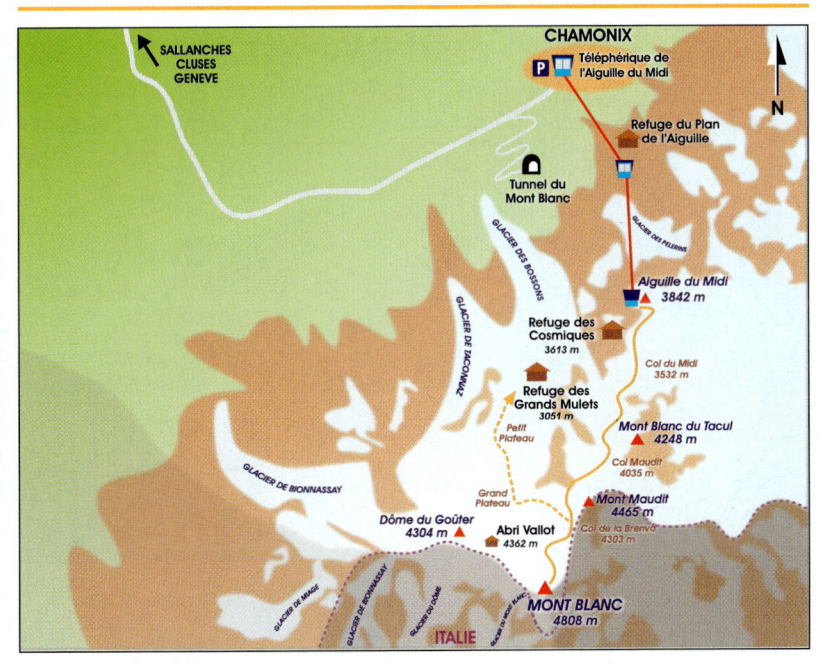

Day 1 = 45 minutes (-200m/+45m)
- Aiguille du Midi Ridge (3775m) -> Cosmiques hut (3613m) = 45mins (-200m/+45m)

Day 2 = 13 hours (+1423 m/-1423 m, +370 m)
- Cosmiques hut (3613m) -> Col du Midi (3532m) = 15mins (- 81m)
- Col du Midi (3532m) -> Shoulder below Mont Blanc du Tacul (4120m) = 2hrs (+588m)
- Shoulder below Mont Blanc du Tacul (4120m) -> Col Maudit (4035m) = 15mins (-85m)
- Col Maudit (4035m) -> Col du Mont Maudit (4345m) = 2hrs 15mins (+310m)
- Col du Mont Maudit (4345m) -> Col de la Brenva (4303m) = 30hrs (-42m/+20m)
- Col de la Brenva (4303m) -> Mur de la Côte (4485m) = 45mins (+182m)
- Mur de la Côte (4485m) -> Mont Blanc (4808m) = 2hrs (+323m)
- Mont Blanc (4808m) -> Aiguille du Midi (3775m) = 5hrs (-1423m/+370m)

GPS

Aiguille du Midi:	Col du mont Maudit:	Mont Blanc:
32T E 0336 034 N 5082 725	32T E 0334 888 N 5079 450	32T E 0334 118 N 5077 668
Cosmiques hut:	Petits Rochers Rouges:	
32T E 0335 873 N 5082 102	32T E 0334 283 N 5078 075	

70 The Three Monts Route

From the Aiguille du Midi to the Cosmiques hut

Aiguille du Midi

Refuge des Cosmiques

① Start point: Aiguille du Midi cable car station, Chamonix-Sud. Car park.

The top station of the Aiguille du Midi cable car is on the northern summit of the mountain. It is connected to the snow tunnels on the southern summit by a footbridge. The left-hand tunnel leads out onto the east-north-east ridge (3775m). This is the ridge that goes down into the upper basin of the Vallée Blanche.

✓ The Cosmiques hut can also be reached from Italy by taking the cable car to Pointe Helbronner and then crossing the Vallée Blanche on foot, or by taking the cable car from Helbronner to the Aiguille du Midi.

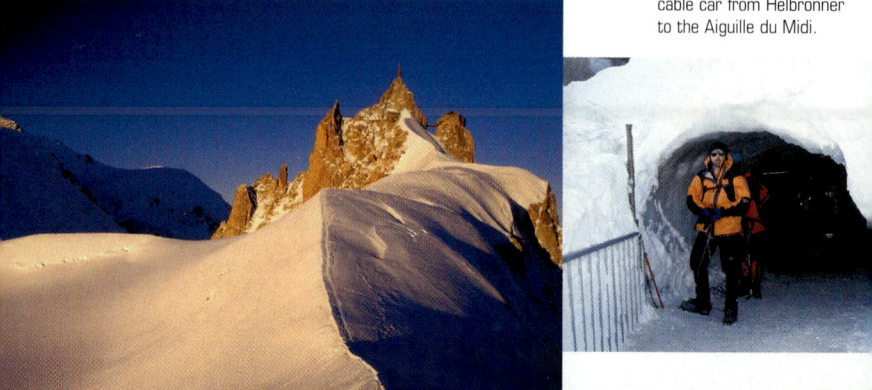

The Three Monts Route | 71

✓ Descending from the Aiguille du Midi can seem easy when the track is well trodden, but the ridge is narrow and quite exposed: crampons and ice axe are necessary. Guides will rope up their clients for this section.

② Descend the East Ridge (3670m). This ridge forms the crest between the impressive north face of the Aiguille de Midi (Chamonix side) and the steep slopes of the south face (Vallée Blanche side). The constant passage of climbers usually produces a good track, but the first few metres can still be quite daunting. The descent requires care and the less experienced may want to use a rope, especially for the first few metres, which are quite steep and narrow. The slope gradually eases until it reaches a flat area (3670 m, 15mins) from where a track forks right towards the Col du Midi. A short detour is often necessary to avoid a bergschrund (3650m), before heading back towards the Col du Midi.

③ Traverse under the South Face of the Aiguille du Midi. A short climb leads to the Cosmiques hut, which sits prominently on a spur of rock (45mins from the Aiguille du Midi).

From the Cosmiques hut to the summit of Mont Blanc

✓ The large bergschrund (at around 3780m) that bars access to the lower slopes below the Tacul can be difficult to cross. It may be necessary to make a large detour to the right through the seracs that dominate the Bossons Glacier, or to climb a several metre-high vertical wall.

④ Go back to the track that goes past the Col du Midi, and then go up through the crevasses and seracs below Mont Blanc du Tacul as far as the shoulder (4100m, 2hrs - 2hrs 30mins).

The conditions and positions of the bergschrund, crevasses and seracs will differ depending on snow conditions and time of year. Sometimes the slope has a uniform covering of hard snow, in which case it is easy to make comfortable steps; at other times, there may be walls of ice and gaping crevasses that are quite difficult to cross.

⑤ From the shoulder below Mont Blanc du Tacul (4120m), descend easy slopes to the Col Maudit (4035m), and then continue towards the north-facing slopes below Mont Maudit (30mins).

The Three Monts Route 73

Mont Blanc — Mont Maudit — Col du mont Maudit

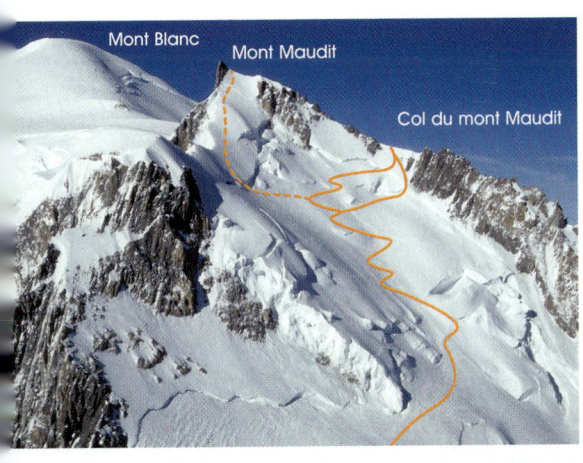

✓ If the bergschrund below the Col du Mont Maudit is too wide to cross, it is possible to go up the steep slopes on the left that lead up to the top of Mont Maudit itself. Traverse right and contour round the summit rocks to get to a slope that leads back to the Col de la Brenva track.

⑥ Go past a line of seracs, and then go straight up the slope to the Col du Mont Maudit (4345m).

⑦ There are two bergschrunds; the first is followed by a short wall, the second by the summit slopes.

⑧ Crossing this second bergschrund sometimes involves some steep and awkward climbing. The final slope up to the Col du Mont Maudit is quite steep for about forty metres and may require roped climbing and the fixing of belays (protruding rocks with in situ pitons, 2hrs - 2hrs 30mins from the shoulder).

74 The Three Monts Route

Mont Maudit
Col du mont Maudit
Col de la Brenva

⑨ From the Col du Mont Maudit, traverse the south-west flank of Mont Maudit, descending slightly, towards the Col de la Brenva (south). Go across a bergschrund, and then climb up to the Col de la Brenva (30mins). If the bergschrund is too wide to cross, climb up to a rise, just below point 4361m, and descend to the Col de la Brenva (4303m) from there.

✓ From the Col de la Brenva, it is possible to escape via the Corridor and reach the Grands Mulets at the Grand Plateau. This provides a quick and useful way of losing altitude in case of problems (weather or physical) (See directions on page 79).

The Three Monts Route

⑩ Climb up the sustained slope of the "Mur de la Cote" (4385m - 4485m, 30-45mins). When the slope is icy, you might need to belay yourself with ice screws for the few meters that are steepest.

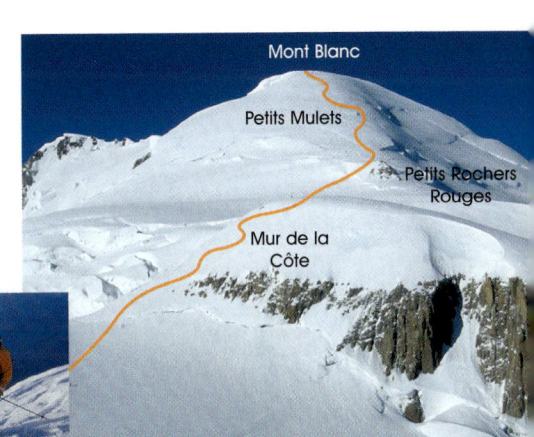

Mont Blanc
Petits Mulets
Petits Rochers Rouges
Mur de la Côte

⑪ Go across a flatter area (south-south-west), and then climb easily up to and around the Petits Rochers Rouges (4577m).

⑫ Climb the summit slopes of Mont Blanc past the Petits Mulets (4690m, 1hr 30mins - 2hrs).

The Three Monts Route

"Paradoxically, it is newcomers to mountaineering who are most attracted to this enterprise. It will undoubtedly be the first time they have climbed at night, by headtorch. They will be nearer than ever to the stars, and the snow crunching beneath their crampons will carry them up towards the light. For the first time, perhaps, they will climb into the sun. Nothing will block their horizon: whichever way they turn and wherever they look, their eyes will shine and their hearts will beat against the walls of their chests."

Jean-Louis Laroche - Florence Lelong
Sommets du Mont Blanc - 1996

The Descent from the Three Monts

⑬ From the summit of Mont Blanc, take a few steps towards Mont Blanc de Courmayeur, and then descend towards the north-northeast, past the rocks of the Petits Mulets (4690m).

⑭ At the Petits Rochers Rouges (4577m), head north-east to get to the top of the Mur de la Côte.
Go down the steep slope of the Mur de la Côte to the Col de la Brenva (4303m).

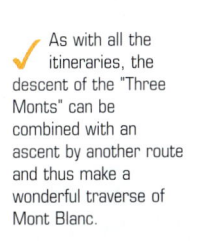

✓ As with all the itineraries, the descent of the "Three Monts" can be combined with an ascent by another route and thus make a wonderful traverse of Mont Blanc.

Mont Maudit

⑮ Go back up to the Col du Mont Maudit (4345m) by traversing across the south-west and west faces of Mont Maudit.

⑯ From the col, descend the north face of Mont Maudit. The first forty metres of the slope are steep and end in a bergschrund.
Sometimes, a wooden stake is placed at the col to provide a belay or abseil anchor.
Belays can also be set up in the rocks that protrude from the middle of the slope, allowing the abseil to be split in two.

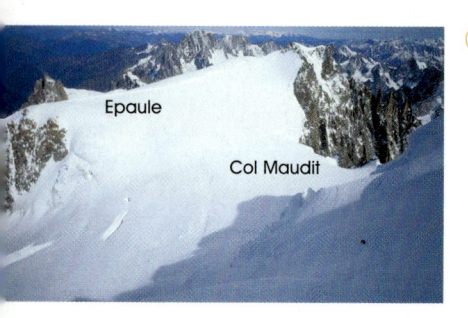

⑰ Descend the second part of the North Face of Mont Maudit (steep sections, crevasses) until it is possible to traverse under the seracs on the right bank of the glacier to reach the Col Maudit (4035m).
From the Col Maudit, go back up to the shoulder below Mont Blanc du Tacul (around 4100m).

⑱ Finally, go down the wide northern slopes of Mont Blanc du Tacul, zigzagging through the crevasses and seracs.
When the bergschrund is too big to cross, most climbers make a detour to the left (west) and go down through the seracs that dominate the Bossons Glacier.
Go past the Col du Midi (3532m) to the foot of the South Face of the Aiguille du Midi.

The Three Monts Route 79

⑲ Go past the South Face (heading north-north-east) to the foot of the North-east Ridge.
Go up the ridge to the cable car station.

ESCAPE ROUTE

From the Col de la Brenva, it may not be advisable (bad weather, extreme fatigue) to go back to the Col du Mont Maudit. In such cases, bear west to go down the Corridor, a long slope that leads to the Grands Mulets Route.

From the Col de la Brenva, head west-north-west to go down gentle slopes cut by a few crevasses.
When the slope steepens, head right (north) to go around a long line of seracs. There are usually one or two crevasses above the Grand Plateau.

Once the slope eases, go up slightly (west) to the Grandes Montées and rejoin the Grands Mulets Route.

Col de la Brenva

Grand Plateau

Climbing up to the Col du Mont Maudit

Pur Alpinisme

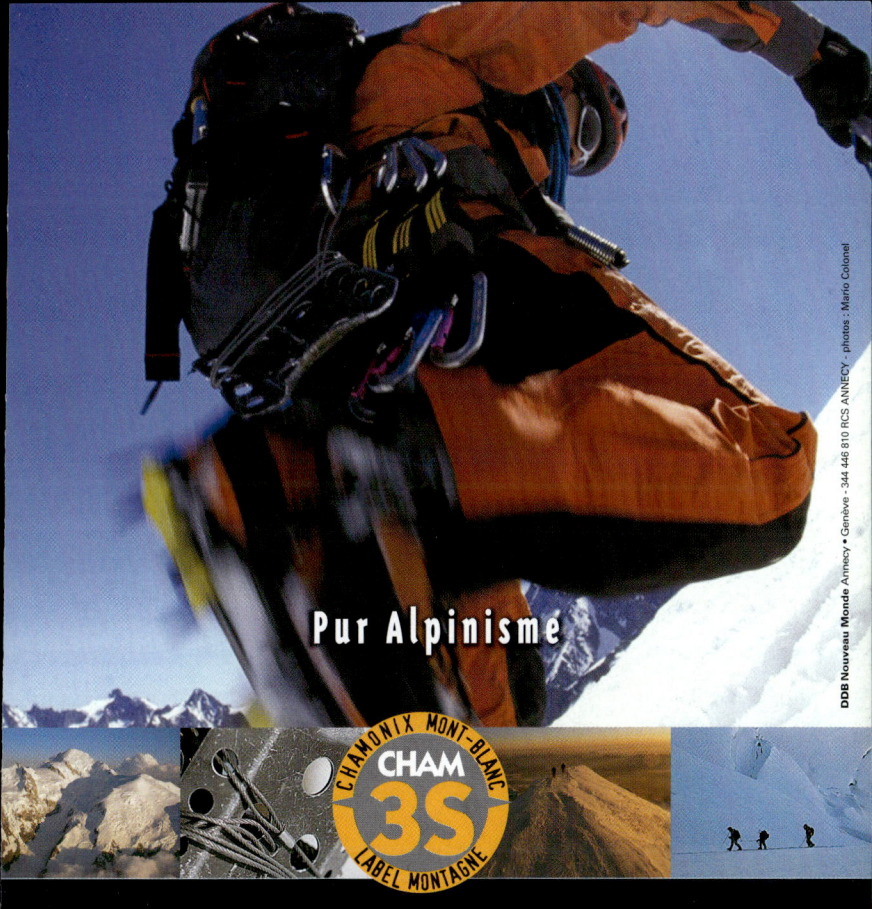

DDB Nouveau Monde Annecy • Genève - 344 446 810 RCS ANNECY - photos : Mario Colonel

CHAMONIX MONT-BLANC
CHAM 3S
LABEL MONTAGNE

COQUOZ Paul & Jean-François Coquoz - 297 & 306, rue Paccard 74400 Chamonix
Tél. : 04 50 53 15 12 - Fax : 04 50 53 25 56 - e-mail : coquoz@cham3s.com

SNELL Olivier & Corinne Snell - 104-118, rue Paccard 74400 Chamonix
Tél. : 04 50 53 02 17 - Fax : 04 50 53 42 40 - e-mail : snell@cham3s.com

SPORTS ALPINS Jacques Luc - 7, place E. Desailloud (face au téléphérique Aig. du Midi)74400 Chamonix
Tél. : 04 50 53 13 60 - Fax : 04 50 53 28 72 - e-mail : sportsalpins@cham3s.com

AMOUDRUZ Bernard Amoudruz - 2, rue Chantemerle (à côté de Botanic) Village Entreprise - 74100 Ville-la-Grand
Tél. : 04 50 87 24 73 - Fax : 04 50 92 66 20 - e-mail : amoudruz@cham3s.com

Catalogue été-hiver on line : (**www.cham3s.com**)

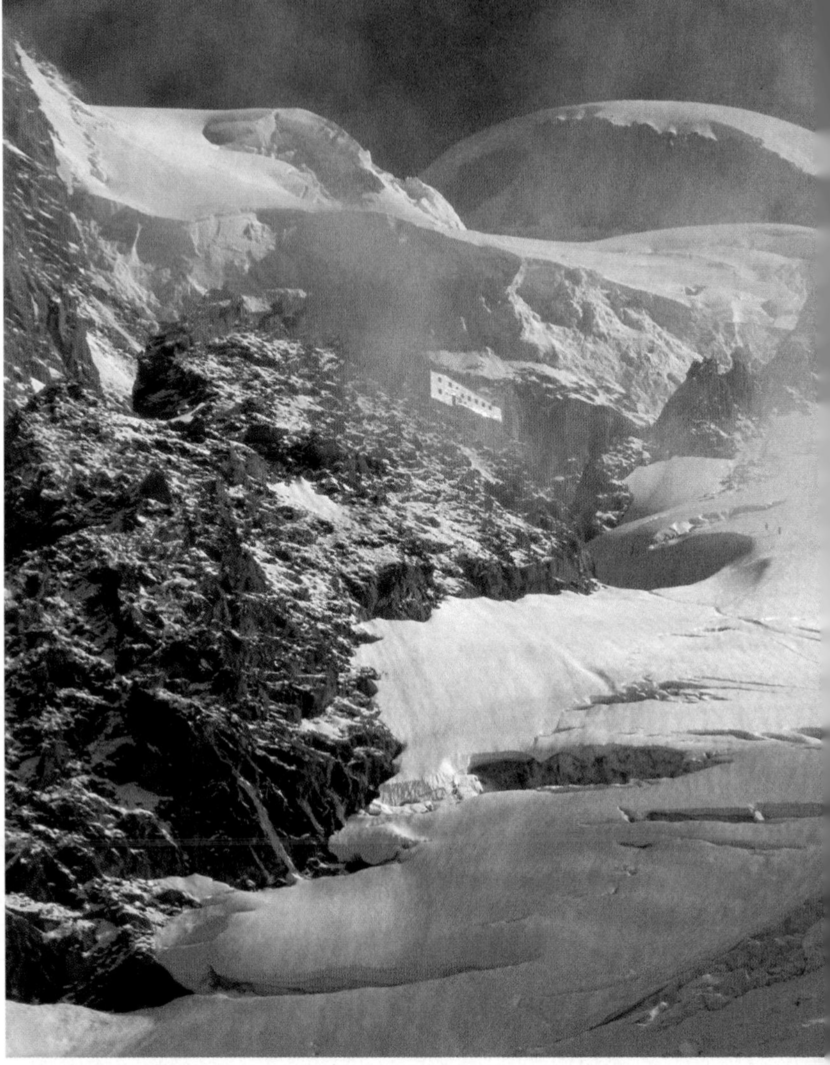

The Grands Mulets Route

The route taken by the first ascenionists in1786

The Grands Mulets Route

The entire route up the Bossons Glacier to the summit can be seen from the Chamonix Valley.

Until about thirty years ago, this was the most popular route to the top of Mont Blanc. It is now used much less frequently, except by skiers in the spring and as a descent route in the summer. It is an excellent route, but very long, especially for the summit day, which starts from the Grands Mulets hut.

CHARACTERISTICS OF THE ROUTE

ADVANTAGES
- Follows in the footsteps of Paccard and Balmat.
- Route is not very crowded.
- Comfortable night at the Grands Mulets hut.
- Extraordinary ambiance during the traverse of the Bossons Glacier.

DISADVANTAGES
- Very long.
- A lot of height gain on the summit day, 1780m.
- Exposed to serac fall during the traverse of the Jonction and the Petit Plateau.

Why "Grands Mulets"?
In his account of the first ascent of Mont Blanc, De Saussure simply described them as a "string of black rocks", so how did they come to be likened to beasts of burden (grands mulets = big mules)? Chamonix scholars think that the word "mulet" comes from "moè", which means "heap" in the local dialect. "Mouè" became "miolet", and then "mulet". Is "heap of rocks" really a suitable name for the bold ridge that slices through the seracs of the Bossons Glacier? "Grands Mulets" is unquestionably much more evocative than "big heap"!

A little history

Mont Blanc conquered

On 7th August 1786, the crystal hunter Jacques Balmat and Doctor Marie-Gabriel Paccard left the Chamonix Valley, reaching the foot of the Montagne de la Côte in the middle of the afternoon. Balmat was carrying a blanket, Paccard a barometer, a pen and a bottle of ink for noting his observations. The two men bivouacked under some large rocks "gîte à Balmat" next to the Bossons Glacier.

At 4:15 on the morning of 8th August they set off again and crossed the Jonction.

At 10 o'clock, they started climbing the Petites Montées.

At 1:50 p.m., they reached the Grand Plateau, then known as the "Valley of Snow". The wind was cold and the climb exhausting. At 3 p.m., the two men hesitated to continue then took over the hard work of breaking trail.

At 3:30, they reached the steep, wide slopes. Balmat was lagging behind, but, spurred on by Paccard, he eventually caught up. Two hours later, the two adventurers were above the Rochers Rouges. The angle of the slope finally eased and the summit appeared to be within reach.

At 6:12, they went past the last rocks, the "Petits Mulets". They reached the summit at 6.23 in the evening.

Route taken during the first ascent according to *"Chamonix et la conquête du Mont-Blanc"*, by Thérèse Robache - 1986.

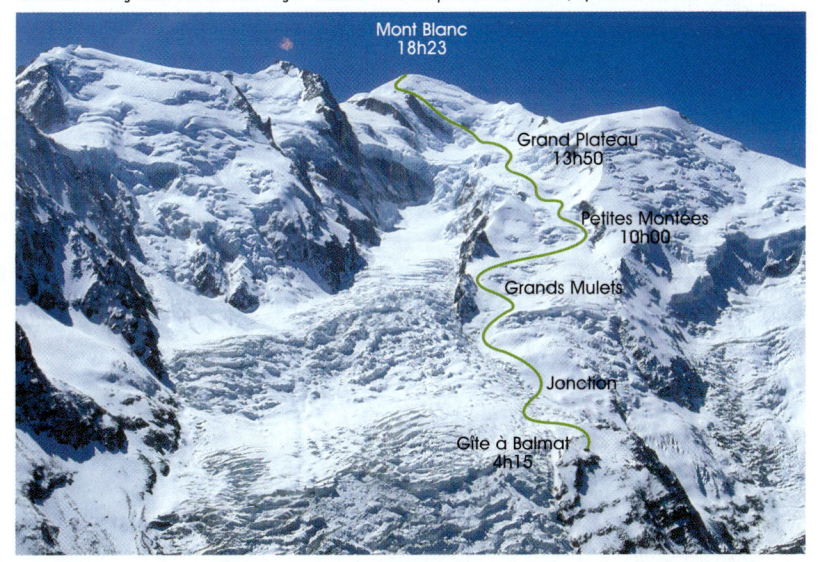

The Mont Blanc Record

The Mont Blanc Record is the fastest time for a round trip to the summit of Mont Blanc from the Place de l'Église in Chamonix. For most of us, climbing Mont Blanc is a tiring two-day expedition. However, some mountaineers, after months of specific training, are capable of doing incredibly fast ascents. The current holder of the record for the round trip Chamonix – Mont Blanc, via the Grands Mulets, is Pierre-André Gobet. His time, 5hrs 10mins 14secs! Here is what he has to say...

What is the record course?

From Chamonix, the course follows the path alongside "La Route Blanche", and then goes up past the entrance to the Mont Blanc Tunnel. From there, it continues to the abandoned cable car station at Les Glaciers, where it picks up the Pierre à l'Échelle path. This path is followed to the Bossons Glacier. It then goes through La Jonction, past the Grands Mulets and up to the Petit Plateau, the Grand Plateau and the Vallot shelter. From the Vallot shelter, the route follows the Bosses Ridge to the summit. The descent follows exactly the same route.

The time for each leg?

3 hours 38 minutes for the climb and 1 hour 32 minutes for the descent.

How did you prepare for such a challenge?

I used the whole winter before the attempt to acclimatise and get fit, mostly running and ski touring with a lot of height gain per day (around 8000m). The first reconnaissance was carried out in the middle of May, "just to see". It was a Sunday afternoon and I went as far as the Petit Plateau, in running shoes. One week before the attempt, I went up to Les Grands Mulets for three days, to acclimatise. During that time, I nipped up to the summit to have a look at the upper section. The crevasses were starting to open up quite seriously.

HISTORICAL OVERVIEW

18th August 1864 – F. Morshead leaves Chamonix at midnight. He reaches the summit at 10:10hrs and gets back to Chamonix at 16:30hrs.

1865 – T.S. Kennedy, Mc Cormick, Charles Hudson and Robert Hadow do a round trip in 16 hours.

1968 - Transition year with a record obtained after specific training. Jean-Marie Bourgeois and René Secrétan reduce the record to 8hrs 48mins.

30th July 1975 - Louis Bailly Bassin brings the record down to 8hrs 10mins. Competition heats up and methods evolve. Runners now have support teams to provide refreshments and equipment.

27th July 1986 - P. Cusin and T. Gazan: 7hrs 56mins.

13th July 1988 - P. Lestas: 6hrs 22mins.

26th July 1988 - L. Smagghe: 5hrs 29mins.

20th July 1990 - Current record: 5hrs 10mins.

The Grands Mulets Route

30th May 2003: a new attempt

Stéphane Brosse and Pierre Gignoux, two ski-mountaineering champions, believe that: "the time for breaking records in running shoes and without equipment is over". They want to set up a new basis for the record by applying the rules of their sport: two-person teams, carrying skis from the start to the finish and roping up for crevassed areas. At first, the two challengers believe that the time taken on skis would be longer than on foot. "You go slower on the way up, and you don't necessarily make up that time during the descent." Stéphane Brosse and Pierre Gignoux started very quickly but lost a little time between La Jonction and the Grands Mulets, where the track was not in optimum condition. Time to reach the summit: 4hrs 04mins, compared with 3hrs 38mins for Pierre-André Gobet. They took three minutes to adjust their gear at the top, and then they descended the north face in 7 minutes! The whole descent took 1hr 8mins, compared with 1hr 32mins for PAG.
Result: 5hrs 15mins. The record was not beaten, but the two athletes are now convinced that a skier can beat a runner in this Mont Blanc challenge.

So, on Friday 20th July 1990…

I left at 5 a.m., to make the best of the cool of the morning and so the ice would be quite hard for the climb but softening up for the descent. I had friends dotted all along the route so that I would always be in visual contact with someone (I had no real desire to end up in a slot!). A hand-line was in place across the crevasse above Les Grands Mulets (it wasn't needed, but it was reassuring to know it was there), as well as a rope up the last part of the Bosses Ridge. I used normal running shoes for the first part, the same ones I use for running on the road, and then changed to track shoes with 18mm spikes when I got to the glacier.

On the way down, I changed back into running shoes at the edge of the glacier.

I got back to the church in Chamonix at 10 o'clock 10 minutes and 14 seconds.

Route description

Mont Blanc
Refuge des Grands Mulets
Plan de l'Aiguille

Route tips

There are two ways to get to the Grands Mulets hut from the Chamonix Valley. The first starts at the Mont-Blanc Tunnel road and follows the path along the right bank of the Bossons Glacier. The second starts at the hamlet of Le Mont and goes up the Montagne de la Côte. Both of these routes are superb and provide breathtaking views. By starting your ascent from the valley and following in the footsteps of the pioneers you will fully appreciate the grandeur of the climb, but the route to the hut is very long and tiring.

Today, it is more usual to use the Aiguille du Midi cable car, which will whisk you up to the Plan de l'Aiguille in ten minutes. From here, a path traverses round to the Bossons Glacier.

The Grands Mulets Route   89

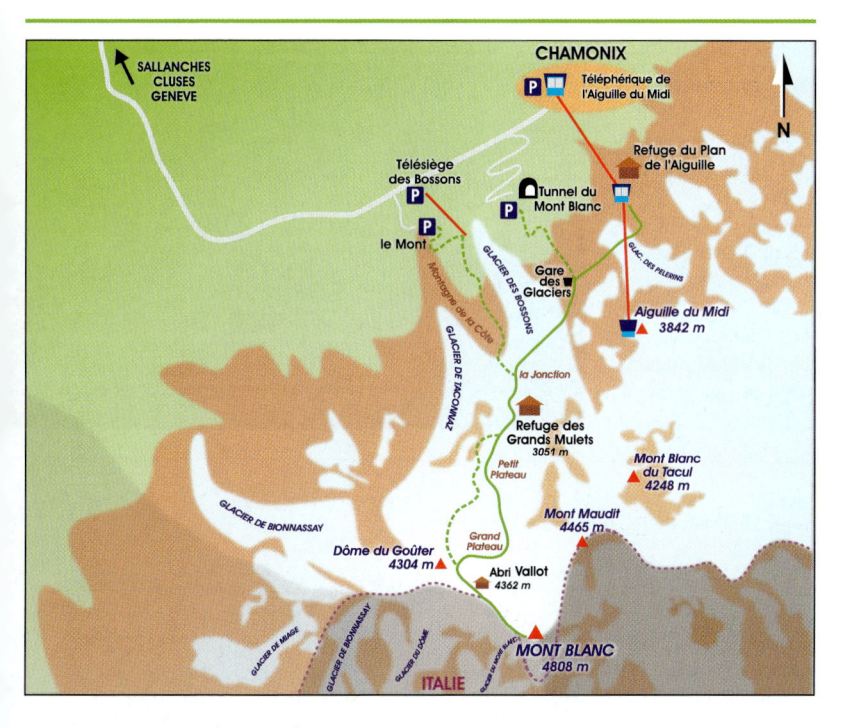

Day 1 = 4 hours (+825m)

- Plan de l'Aiguille (2310m) -> Les Glaciers disused cable car station (2414m) = 1hr (+104m)
- Les Glaciers disused cable car station (2414m) -> Grands Mulets hut (3057m) = 3hrs (+721m/-78m)

Day 2 = 13 hours (+1829 m/-2575 m)

- Grands Mulets hut (3057m) -> Petit Plateau (3650m) = 2hrs (+593m)
- Petit Plateau (3650m) -> Grand Plateau (3980m) = 1hr 30mins (+330m)
- Grand Plateau (3980m) -> Col du Dôme (4255m) = 1hr (+275m)
- Col du Dôme (4255m) -> Mont Blanc (4808m) = 2hrs 30mins (+553m)
- Mont Blanc (4808m) -> Plan de l'Aiguille (2310m) = 6hrs (-2576m/+78m)

GPS

Plan de l'Aiguille:	Grands Mulets hut:
32T E 0335 914 N 5085 288	32T E 0335 053 N 5083 782
Les Glaciers station:	Mont Blanc:
32T E 0333 955 N 5081 438	32T E 0334 118 N 5077 668

The Grands Mulets Route

APPROACH TO THE GRANDS MULETS HUT

There are three ways of getting to the hut:
- From the Plan de l'Aiguille, reached by the Aiguille du Midi cable car.
- From the Mont Blanc Tunnel car park, via the disused cable car station at Les Glaciers.
- From le Mont, via the Montagne de la Côte.

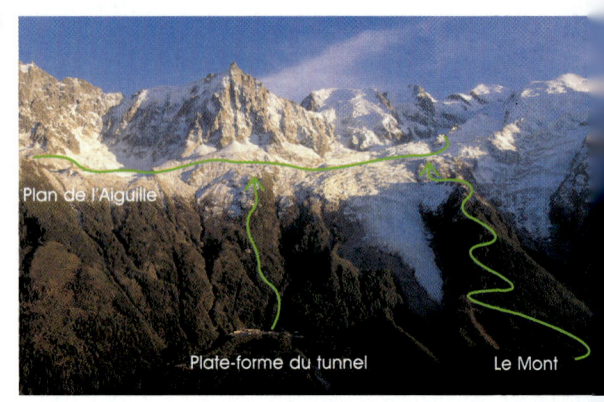

From the Plan de l'Aiguille (2310m)

① From the Aiguille du Midi half-way station (2310m), follow the path along the moraine on the right bank of the Pélerins Glacier (red marks) to get to the Plan Glacier at around 2400 m. Traverse the rock covered glacier horizontally, and then go up the moraine on the left bank to get to a path that contours round to the disused cable car station at Les Glaciers (2414m). The path continues above the Pierre à l'Échelle to reach the right bank of the Bossons Glacier at around 2500 m.

② Just before the Bossons Glacier, a shelter has been roughly hewn out of the mountainside to provide protection from stones falling from the Aiguille du Midi.

✓ Both the flow rate of the Bossons Glacier and the average angle of the slope between Mont Blanc and the valley are very high. The combination of these two factors means that this immense icefall is constantly changing. The route through the Jonction, the Côte des Grands Mulets and Les Cerisiers changes every day.

③ Cross the Plan Glacier, winding your way through the seracs and crevasses, to get to the Jonction.

④ Go up the Côte des Grands Mulets to get to the southernmost point of the Grands Mulets rocks. The hut is perched on the rocks (cable for climbing the last twenty metres).

OTHER ROUTES TO THE GRANDS MULETS HUT

Starting from Le Mont
Magnificent approach following in the footsteps of the first ascensionists.
Two possibilities:
- Car park for the glacier chairlift (1025m). Take the chairlift, which stops 25m below the chalet-refreshments stand (1400m). From here, follow the Jonction path.
- Car park (1198m) at the hamlet of Le Mont, just before the Olympic ski jump (where the Jonction path starts).

✓ Before going up to the Grands Mulets hut via the Montagne de la Côte, it is essential to find out about the state of the Bossons Glacier. When there are good snow-bridges over the crevasses the traverse is quite straightforward, but, as summer progresses and the snow melts, the route gradually becomes impracticable.

Follow a good path to the café at the Chalet du Glacier des Bossons, and then continue along the path to the Chalet des Pyramides (breathtaking views of the glacier icefalls).

The Grands Mulets Route | 93

Take the path up to Mont Corbeau. Traverse onto the eastern side of the mountain and follow the path across several steep slopes and through the cliffs (yellow marks).

Go past the "Gîte à Balmat" to reach the Jonction just below the top of the Montagne de la Côte (4hrs, 2589m).

Go onto the glacier and cross the Jonction to get to the Côte des Grands Mulets. Climb this slope to the hut (2hrs, total from the car parks = 6hrs).

From the tunnel car park (1270m)
This is the standard route to or from the hut when the Aiguille du Midi cable car is closed.
Start at the "Crémerie du Cerro" car park. When going up to the tunnel, this is on the right, just before the tollbooths.
The path follows the right bank of the Torrent de la Creuse, goes past the disused intermediate cable car station at La Para, and then up to the disused cable car station at Les Glaciers (4hrs). From here, the route follows the route from the Plan de l'Aiguille (see p.90).

The Grands Mulets Route

From the Grands Mulets hut to Mont Blanc via the Petit and Grand Plateaux

The Grands Mulets hut
Since 1853, a number of huts and "hostelries" have been built on the rocks of the Grands Mulets, superseding the original "Saussure shelter".
1866: construction of the Pavillon, at the initiative of the guide Sylvain Couttet and the mayor of Chamonix.
1896: construction of a new "hostelry", which lasted until the French Alpine Club built a new prefabricated metal hut in 1959/1960. This hut is still in use.

(5) From just below the hut, cross the slope (towards the south-west), and then, at around 3155m, climb a steep slope (known as the Côte des Cerisiers or the Petites Montées) to get to the Petit Plateau (3650 m, 2hrs).

(6) Falling seracs make the Petit Plateau a dangerous place. To minimise the risk, you must move as quickly as possible until you are out of the danger zone (the crossing should take no more than about 30 minutes).

The Grands Mulets Route | 95

Mont Blanc — Dôme du Goûter

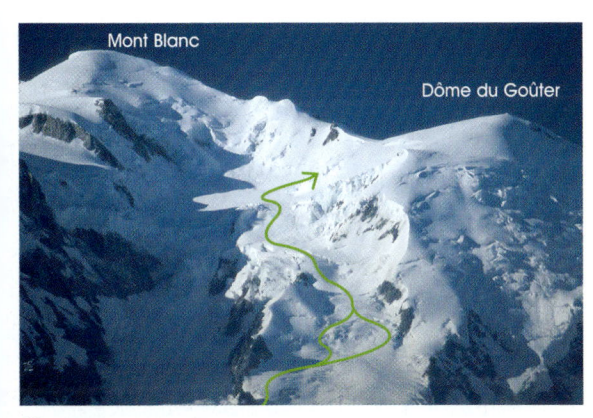

⑦ Go up a second steep slope, Les Grandes Montées, at the top of which there is often a wide crevasse.

✓ In 1799, Ascension (first name given as a homage to the first ascent of Mont Blanc) Elie de Montgolfier (nephew of the Montgolfier brothers) climbed as far as the Petites Montées. For a boy of seventeen with very little experience of the mountains this was a truly remarkable feat.

Abri Vallot — Dôme du Goûter — Grand PLateau

⑧ Cross the Grand Plateau.
The route curves round to the south-west to join the Goûter Route between the Col du Dôme and the Vallot shelter.

☞ **Insert end of Goûter Route p.53**

Alternative access to Mont Blanc by the North Ridge of the Dôme

Because of the danger from falling seracs during the crossing of the Petit Plateau, the route via the North Ridge of the Dôme du Goûter has become increasingly popular during the last few years.

It is a superb Alpine route, with a very airy atmosphere. The concave slopes that lead to the Dôme Ridge are precipitously perched on top of the cliffs above the Taconnaz Glacier. This perfectly etched ridge, a proud buttress magnificently set above the Petites Montées, catches the eye, even from the floor of the valley.

However, the route should not be undertaken lightly. It crosses much steeper ground than the standard route and there are often sections of hard ice, which require good ice climbing skills to overcome. As it makes a detour over the Dôme du Goûter, the route is also much longer. The North Ridge of the Dôme is a highly recommendable route, but it is much more difficult than the classic route via the Montées and the Plateaux.

The Grands Mulets Route 97

5 a From the Grands Mulets hut, head north-west across the glacier. At around 3165 m, traverse horizontally rightwards, leaving the classic route via the Plateaux on your left. Follow a gentle slope to reach the steeper slopes that mark the foot of the Dôme Ridge between two small rocky spurs (3210m).

6 a Climb the slopes that form the North Ridge of the Dôme (south).

7 a Two bergschrunds, the first at 3535m, the second at 3655m, are usually crossed on the right. Skiers generally take their skis off here and put them on their rucksacks.

98 The Grands Mulets Route

> ✓ Once the snow has melted and ice starts to show through, it may be necessary to pitch the steeper sections of the ridge. Ice screws will then be necessary.

⑧ a Climb the sustained slope above, often ice, coming back close to the arête. After about 150m, where the slope eases, head towards the summit of the Dôme (south-west) and join the Goûter Route just before the Col du Dôme (5hrs).

☛ **Insert end of Goûter Route p.53**

The Grands Mulets Route 99

> *"When he got to this height he saw underneath him all the snowy points of mountains and rivers of ice shining like diamonds – the whole country of Switzerland, Savoy and part of Piedmont, the lake of Geneva – and the sky appeared to him of a deep Prussian blue – but what delighted him most was to distinguish, which he had the happiness of doing, his wife and sons at Chamonix where he had left them, waving a flag, which was the signal he agreed they should make if they saw him and knew he was safe."*
>
> About the ascent of De Saussure.
> **Georgiana, Duchess of Devonshire**
> Letter to her daughter - 1792

100 The Grands Mulets Route

DESCENT VIA THE GRANDS MULETS

⑨ From the summit, descend the Bosses Ridge and the slope under the Vallot shelter (see Goûter Route, p.57).

⑩ Just before the Col du Dôme, turn right from the Goûter Route to go down to the Grand Plateau.
There is usually a big crevasse to go round. The initial slopes, down to the Grandes Montées, are quite gentle.

Col du Dôme

Grand Plateau

⑪ Descending the Grandes Montées does not usually pose any particular problems.

The Grands Mulets Route 101

Col du Dôme
Petit Plateau
Grands Mulets

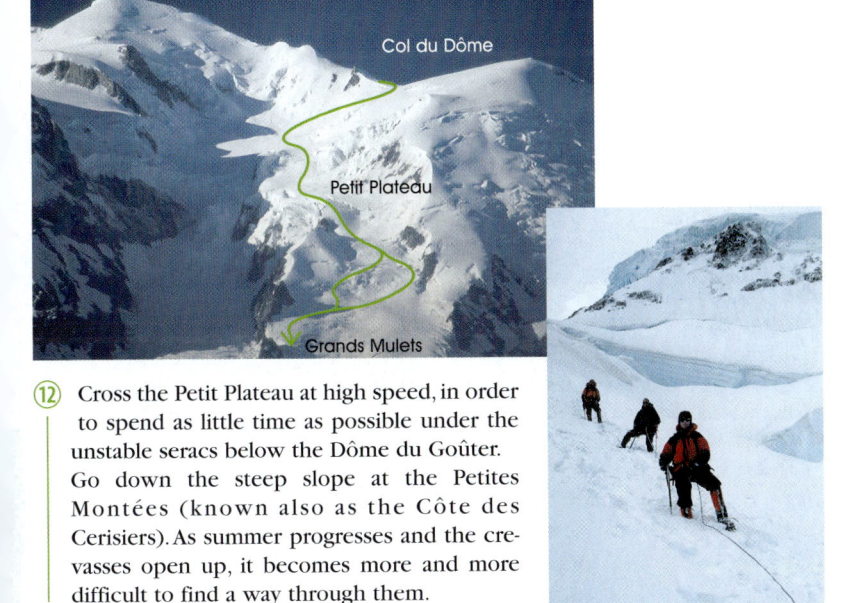

⑫ Cross the Petit Plateau at high speed, in order to spend as little time as possible under the unstable seracs below the Dôme du Goûter. Go down the steep slope at the Petites Montées (known also as the Côte des Cerisiers). As summer progresses and the crevasses open up, it becomes more and more difficult to find a way through them.

⑬ When this route becomes impracticable, it is possible to traverse rightwards and climb Pic Wilson (or Rocher Pitschner) and follow an elegant ridge down to the hut.

102 The Grands Mulets Route

⑭ Descend beside the rocks of the Grands Mulets, and then go down the sustained slope on the right to reach the Jonction.

⑮ When the slope eases, work your way eastwards, and more or less horizontally, across the Plan Glacier, at first winding through the crevasses and seracs, and then more easily.

⑯ Leave the right bank of the glacier (at around 2525m) to follow the Pierre à l'Échelle path (beware of stone fall from the Aiguille du Midi). Traverse horizontally at first, and then go up slightly to reach a good path near the disused cable car station at Les Glaciers.

From here:
- Go back to the Plan de l'Aiguille cable car station by following the path that contours round the base of the Aiguille du Midi before cutting across the flat part of the Pélerins Glacier.
- Go straight down to the valley along the path that follows the line of the disused cable car.

MONT BLANC ON SKIS

The Grands Mulets Route is the classic way of doing Mont Blanc on skis. The terrain is perfect for "skinning-up" on skis and the sustained slopes provide a wonderful descent. Most skiers leave their skis at the Vallot shelter and climb the Bosses Ridge in crampons. The Bosses Ridge is not usually very pleasant to ski, as the snow is generally wind-packed and the descent is very exposed. Only extremely good skiers who intend to do a direct descent of the North Face take their skis to the top.

Depending on the weather and snow conditions, Mont Blanc can be skied as early as March. And of course the descent, which can seem very long and often tedious on foot, becomes a real pleasure on skis.

Although it is not particularly difficult to ski Mont Blanc, it does require a certain amount of ski touring experience. Some sections can be quite tricky (crossing the Pierre à l'Échelle, winding through the seracs at the Jonction, skiing the crevassed slopes of the Petites and Grandes Montées) and skiing at more than 4000m requires a good pair of lungs and strong thighs!

104 The Grands Mulets Route

Ski-ing itinerary

From where you arrive by cable car at the Plan de l'Aiguille, the ski track usually goes down about 10 meters into a small bowl which runs alongside the right bank of the moraine of the Pelerins Glacier. Go up the glacier for a short distance, and then traverse around the foot of the Aiguille du Midi (at around 2500m). Warning: the Gazex avalanche triggering systems, situated a little lower (at the level of the summer path) are regularly used to dislodge accumulations of snow on the slopes above the entrance to the Mont Blanc tunnel.

Go above (2560m) the disused cable car station at Les Glaciers and descend slightly as soon as the Bossons Glacier is reached (2525m). Depending on the snow conditions, this traverse can be quite delicate.

Once on the glacier, the ski route is identical to the classic itinerary described above.

✓ All of the "Grands Mulets" routes can be done on skis.
- The North Ridge of the Dôme provides a magnificent exposed and sustained (40/45°) descent that will satisfy even the most demanding of skiers and the Dôme du Goûter is a respectable objective in its own right.
- The traverse of the Jonction to get to the Montagne de la Côte is a worthwhile but rarely done ski tour that involves some interesting route finding.
- A return cable car trip, from the Plan de l'Aiguille, can be avoided by descending directly from the disused cable car station at Les Glaciers to the tunnel entrance. Again this offers superb skiing and a very long descent... when there is enough snow.

Les Houches
l'autre voie pour découvrir Le Mont Blanc
the other way to discover

The Carlaveyron nature reserve and other environmentally protected sites, offer walkers an unspoilt countryside.

Mountain bike trails are accessible from the top of the lift systems.

MONT-BLANC - 4810 m
LES HOUCHES 1007 m
CHAMONIX MONT-BLANC - 1035 m

We strongly advise everyone wishing to attempt the ascent of Mont-Blanc, to hire the services of a professional mountain guide.

- Discover the Mont-Blanc massif as safely as possible with the mountain guides and trekking guides from Les Houches.
  - The Tourist Office is here to help you prepare your holiday in the 'Pays du Mont-Blanc'.
    - Hotels, gîtes, guest houses and rentals can be booked at our Reservation Centre.
      - Four seasons : numerous sporting activities or leisure and cultural events all year round.

Tourist Office
Office de tourisme
Place de la mairie - BP 9 - 74310 Les Houches
Tél. : **04 50 55 50 62** / Fax : **04 50 55 53 16**
info@leshouches.com - www.leshouches.com

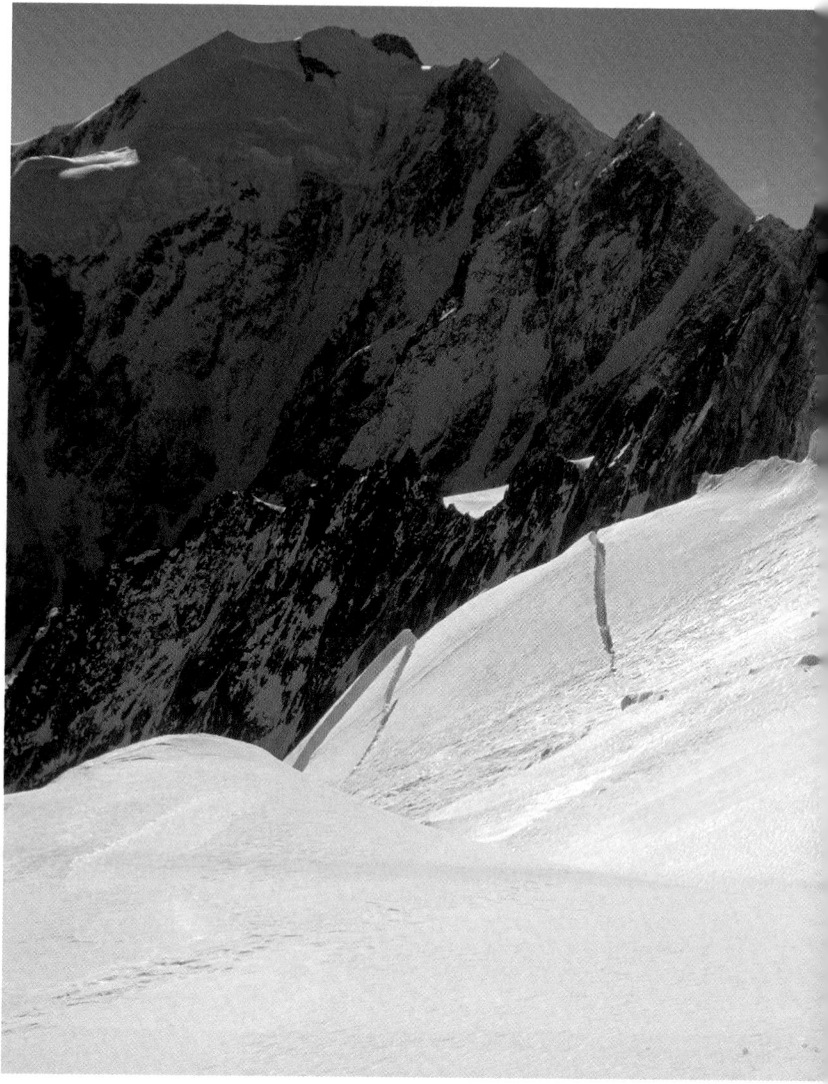

The Pope Route

The Italian ordinary route: hidden and wild

The Pope Route

The ordinary route on the Italian side of Mont Blanc sees very little traffic. All the better!
The itinerary follows the little known Miage and Dôme Glaciers through the heart of a wild and unspoilt corner of the massif.

The Pope Route, tucked away at the end of Val Veny and hidden from the cable cars of Chamonix and Courmayeur, winds a secret path through the secluded architecture of Mont Blanc's impressive South-West Face. Far from the beaten track and a route that most people have never even seen, this is Mont Blanc for the more adventurous climber. Setting foot on the Miage Glacier, with its enormous moraines, will give you a real foretaste of the greater ranges; so much so that some climbers refer to the Val Veny as a "mini-Himalaya".
The route is long, both in terms of height gain and distance, but this should not deter the fit and competent climber as, technically, it is no harder than the Goûter or Grands Mulets Routes. And, as for any high altitude experience, the emotion and pleasure are even more intense when you are away from the madding crowds.

.

CHARACTERISTICS OF THE ROUTE

ADVANTAGES
- One of the wildest corners of Mont Blanc.
- Few other climbers.
- Technical difficulties similar to those of the Goûter Route.
- Hut at a reasonable altitude, thereby limiting the effects of altitude sickness.
- Only route on the Italian side at this level of difficulty.

DISADVANTAGES
- A lot of distance to be covered.
- A lot of height gain: 1371m the first day, 1739m the second day.
- Highly crevassed and complex glacial terrain.
- Logistics if descend on the French side.

A little history

The high mountain Pope (1857 - 1939)

Italian, mountaineer, priest, professor of theology, director of the Ambrosia Library in Milan, and of the Vatican Library, Achille Ratti was elected cardinal in 1921. The following year he was crowned Pope, under the name Pius XI. The signature of the Lateran Accords with Mussolini, which ensured the independence of the Vatican, and of a concordat with eighteen countries, including Germany, made Pius XI a controversial figure. In the Lateran Accords, the Italian State made important concessions to the Vatican, but they also gave Mussolini a great deal of prestige. From then on, the head of the Catholic Church was irrevocably associated with Il Duce. Pius XI described Mussolini as "a man of Providence".

However, as early as 1926, Achille Ratti had written an encyclical condemning the extreme rightwing group Action Française and, in 1937, he condemned the excesses of Nazi Germany in an encyclical that was smuggled into Germany to be read on Palm Sunday from the pulpits of churches all over the country. In May 1938, when Hitler visited Rome, the Pope left Castel Gondolfo, saying, "The air here is not good for me..." Just before his death, he started preparing the Humani Generis Unitas encyclical, which condemned racism and Nazism. History remembers him as a Pope who defended human rights at a time when fascist propaganda permeated all aspects of life, including mountaineering. The cardinal was an experienced mountaineer whose climbs included a new route on the Pointe Dufour of Monte Rosa, in 1885, and an ascent of the Matterhorn, in 1889. That same year, he became the first Italian to traverse Monte Rosa from Macugnaga to Zermatt. In August 1890, he turned his attention to Mont Blanc. After spending the night in the Vallot Observatory, then under construction, he and his companions, the two Bonin brothers, Luigi Graselli, Joseph Gadin and Alexis Proment, descended the Italian side of the mountain. Their obvious but elegant route, via the Dome du Goûter, the South ridge of the Aiguilles Grises and the Dome Glacier, was to become the Italian ordinary route or the "Pope Route".

> *"True mountaineering is not about dare-devil feats, on the contrary, it is entirely a question of prudence and a little bravery, of strength and steadfastness, of a feeling for nature and her most hidden beauties, which are sometimes terrible, but more sublime and more fertile for the spirit that contemplates them."*
>
> **Achille Ratti**
> Climbs on Alpine Peak - 1923

The Pope Route

Route description

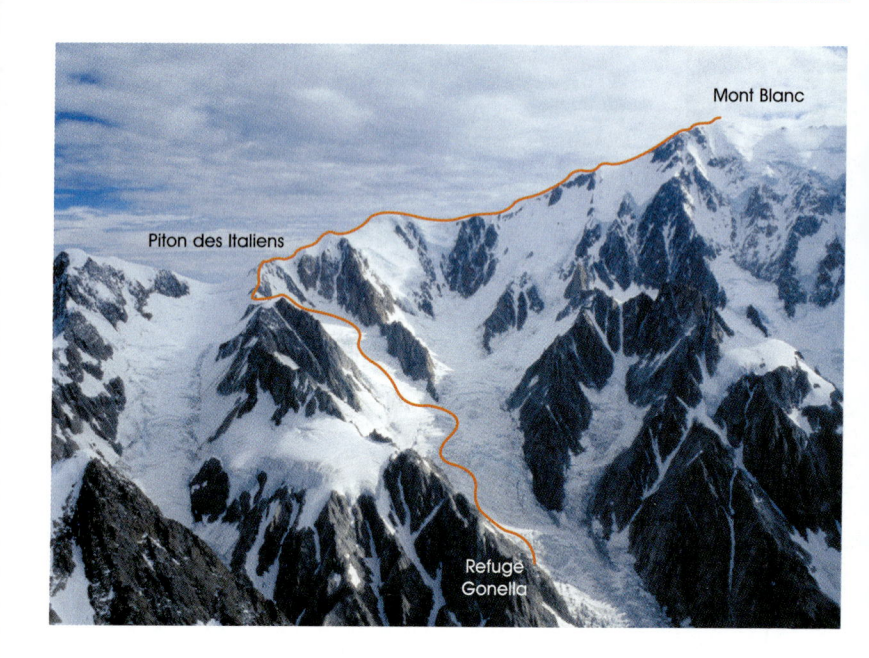

Route tips

Experienced mountaineers will always preach the gospel of the early start! By leaving early, you can climb at a comfortable pace and still have time to take breaks when you need them.

It is a long way from Val Veny to the top of the Miage Glacier. If you are not in a rush, you will be able to take a relaxed lunch break before starting up the Aiguilles Grises and enjoy the fabulous glacial scenery around you. If the approach to the hut is done at a gentle pace, you won't waste precious energy; energy you will undoubtedly need for the climb to the summit the following day.

By leaving the hut while it is still dark, you will have good snow conditions on the glacier and enough daylight to get to the top and back down to the valley the same day.

The Pope Route

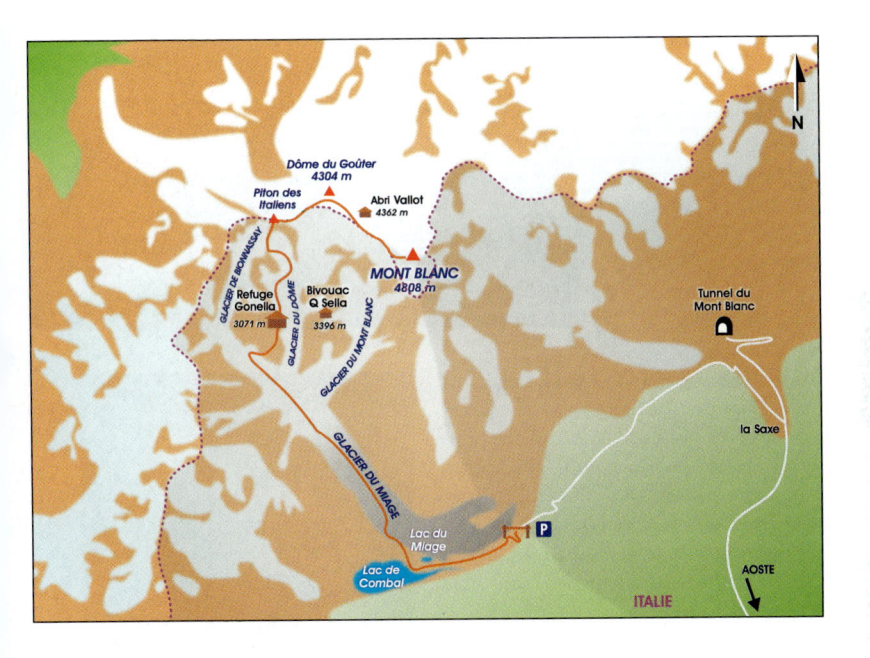

Day 1 = 5 hours (+1371m)

- Car park (1700m) -> Bar Combal (1968m) = 1hr (+268m)
- Bar Combal (1968m) -> Aiguilles Grises path (2620m) = 2hrs 30mins (+652m)
- Aiguilles Grises path (2620m) -> Gonella hut (3071m) = 1hr 30mins (+451m)

Day 2 = 13 hours (+1737m/-3108m)

- Gonella hut (3071m) -> Piton des Italiens (4002m) = 3hrs (+931m)
- Piton des Italiens (4002m) -> Vallot shelter (4362m) = 1hr 30mins (+360m)
- Vallot shelter (4362m) -> Mont Blanc (4808m) = 2hrs (+446m)
- Mont Blanc (4808m) -> Val Veny (1700m) = 6hrs 30mins (-3108m)

GPS

Start of Aiguilles Grises path: 32T E 0331 125 N 5075 690	Piton des Italiens: 32T E 0331 475 N 5078 255	Mont Blanc: 32T E 0334 118 N 5077 668
Gonella hut: 32T E 0331 615 N 5076 255	Vallot shelter: 32T E 0333 185 N 5078 418	

112 The Pope Route

**FROM VAL VENY
TO THE GONELLA HUT**

Start point:
Val Veny. Car park at the barrier (around 1700m). The road after the barrier has been swept away by a landslide.

① Follow the road to Lac Combal. Just before the bridge across the River Doire (1950m) and turn right onto the track that goes up to the Lac du Miage. Follow the path behind Bar Combal (old car park, 1hr), and then, after a small plateau, go up the side of the moraine and onto its crest.

② Follow the crest of the moraine (yellow paint marks). At the end of the moraine, continue up the Miage Glacier - the ice is completely hidden by rocks. Work your way towards the middle of the glacier (cairns, yellow paint marks).

The Pope Route | 113

③ Go up the glacier to the foot of the Aiguilles Grises (2600 m, 2hrs 30mins). This is where the Bionnassay Italien Glacier and Dôme Glacier meet.

Go a short distance up the right bank of the Bionnassay Glacier. At around 2620m, turn right onto the path that goes up the Aiguilles Grises. The path is to the left of the lowest point of the ridge, at the bottom of a large snow cone at the foot of a characteristic Y-shaped gully.

The path crosses the base of the Aiguilles Grises to get to the large snowfield on the right bank of the Dôme Glacier (yellow paint marks).

④ From the glacier, head rightwards across an area of muddy scree, followed by a small snowfield and a roche moutonnée (chain). Cross a small stream, go over another snowfield and past a spring to get to a sort of small col.

⑤ A series of tight hairpin bends leads to a horizontal traverse across a landslide.

Climb a small cliff using the in-situ ladder and chains.

114 The Pope Route

⑥ Go across a second landslide to reach a ridge.

✓ Two glaciers with the same name? In fact, the "French" glacier is called the "Glacier de Miage"; the "Italian" glacier is the "Glacier du Miage".

⑦ The path goes up a small scree slope and across a snowfield to reach the moraine beside the large snowfield on the right bank of the Dôme Glacier. The hut can be clearly seen from here. Go diagonally across the snowfield (northeast) to get to and climb the rocky slope on which the hut is situated (1hr 30mins). 5hrs from the Val Veny car park.

From the Gonella hut to the Col des Aiguilles Grises

⑧ From the hut, head north to cross a series of small snowfields and rocky areas (be careful at the beginning of the season, the slopes are steep and exposed above cliffs). Check out the route to the glacier in daylight when you get to the hut.

Glacier du Dôme

⑨ Go up very slightly to go through a small notch, and then go down a steep snowfield to get to the Dôme Glacier (3085 m, 15mins).

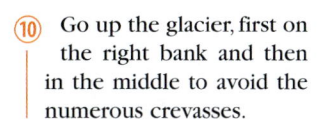

⑩ Go up the glacier, first on the right bank and then in the middle to avoid the numerous crevasses.

The Pope Route

⑪ Climb the slope that leads to the upper basin, which is bounded by the Tour/Calotte/Col des Aiguilles Grises on one side, and the cliffs of the southern buttress of the Dôme du Goûter on the other (1hr 45mins, 2hrs from the hut).

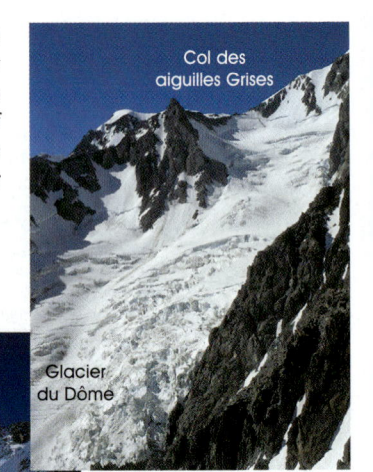

Col des aiguilles Grises

Glacier du Dôme

✓ At the end of the summer season, when there are too many crevasses to go up the Dôme Glacier, it is possible to climb the South Ridge of the Aiguilles Grises directly from the Gonella hut, and then traverse across towards the Col des Aiguilles Grises.

⑫ Cross the bergschrund and climb the snow slope that leads to the Col des Aiguilles Grises (it is possible, given the right conditions, to get back onto the Aiguilles Grises Ridge closer to the rounded ridge that comes down from the Piton des Italiens).

From the Col des Aiguilles Grises to Mont Blanc

⑬ From the Col des Aiguilles Grises, contour round the Bionnassay side of a small rock pillar and then climb the snowy ridge to the Piton des Italiens (4002m, 1hr, 3hrs from the hut).

⑭ Follow the narrow Bionnassay Ridge (cornices on the French side) to the Dôme du Goûter. Stay to the right of the summit to get to the Col du Dôme, and then the Vallot shelter (1hr 30mins). The route to the summit from the Bosses Ridge is the same as the Goûter Route.

☞ **Insert Goûter Route description from p.53**

The Pope Route

"It was a little time before I could look at anything steadily. I wanted the whole panorama condensed into one point... The morning was most lovely, there was not even a wreath of mist coming up from the valley.
One of our guides had been up nine times, and he said he had never seen such weather. But with this extreme clearness of atmosphere, there was a filmy look about the peaks, merging into a perfect haze of distance in the valleys. All the great points in the neighbourhood of Chamouni – the Buet, the Aiguille Verte, the Col du Bonhomme, and even the Bernese Alps – were standing forth clearly enough; but the other second class mountains were mere ridges."

Albert Smith
Mont Blanc -1852

The Pope Route | 119

Descent via the Pope Route

⑮ From the summit of Mont Blanc, go down the Bosses Ridge to the Col du Dôme (see Goûter Route, p.57).

⑯ At the Col du Dôme, leave the track from the Bosses Ridge to the Goûter hut to contour round to the left of the summit of the Dôme du Goûter. When going around the summit, be careful not to stray too far left onto the very steep slopes of the south face.

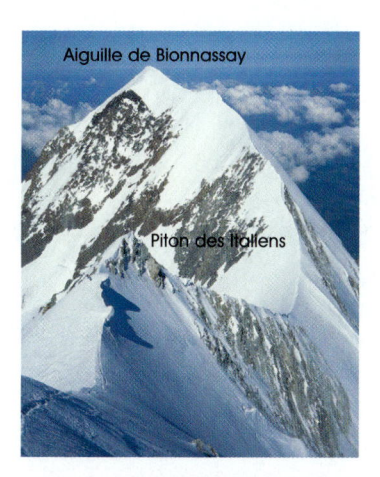

Abri Vallot

Aiguille de Bionnassay

Piton des Italiens

⑰ Go down the Bionnassay Ridge (heading southwest) to the Piton des Italiens (4002m), narrow sections.

The Pope Route

⑱ Leave the Bionnassay Ridge to descend southwards down the Aiguilles Grises Ridge (alternating bands of snow and rock).

Go rightwards around a small rock peak to get to the Col des Aiguilles Grises (3810m). Head left (east) and go down a short slope to cross the bergschrund and reach the western branch of the Dôme Glacier.

⑲ Cross this basin, and then go down the middle of the glacier (crevasses) past the foot of a tower of rock on the South Ridge of the Dôme du Goûter.

⑳ Go down the glacier, avoiding the areas of crevasses as best you can, to the small plateau at the foot of the gully that leads up to the Quintino Sella bivouac shelter.

The Pope Route

㉑ Via this plateau, move back onto the right bank of the glacier. At around 3085m, go up a short snowfield to get onto the broken rocks of the right bank.

✓ Perched on a rocky ridge at the foot of the Aiguilles Grises, on the right bank of the Dôme Glacier, the Gonella hut is not easy to see. It is visible when coming down the upper part of the glacier.

㉒ Go over a small col to get to the hut.
(From the Col du Dôme to the hut: 3hrs).

The Pope Route

DESCENT FROM THE GONELLA HUT TO VAL VENY

(23) From the hut, follow the path that goes steeply down the cliff (yellow paint marks, cables) to the large snowfield on the right bank of the Dôme Glacier. Cross this snowfield diagonally rightwards (south-west) to get to the moraine.
Still heading rightwards, cross a second snowfield to reach a path that leads to a poorly defined ridge.

(24) Cross the landslides (in-situ cables) and use the in-situ cables and ladder to descend the steep ground that follows.
Traverse across an area of unstable ground and go down a series of tight hairpins to a sort of small col.

The Pope Route 123

㉕ Follow the path to the Bionnassay Italien Glacier, crossing a number of little streams, snowfields and roches moutonnées (chains) before reaching more muddy ground.
Follow the Bionnassay Italien Glacier to get to the Miage Glacier, going round a number of large crevasses.

㉖ Go down the middle of the long, flat Miage Glacier.

㉗ Go up to the crest of the right bank moraine to get to the path that leads to Bar Combal and the Val Veny road. (From the Gonella hut to the Val Veny car park: 2hrs 30mins).

124 The Pope Route

On the Bosses Ridge

COMPAGNIE des GUIDES
SAINT-GERVAIS MONT-BLANC

tradition et passion

Tél. +33 (0)4 50 47 76 55

since **1864**

www.guides-mont-blanc.com
info@guides-mont-blanc.com

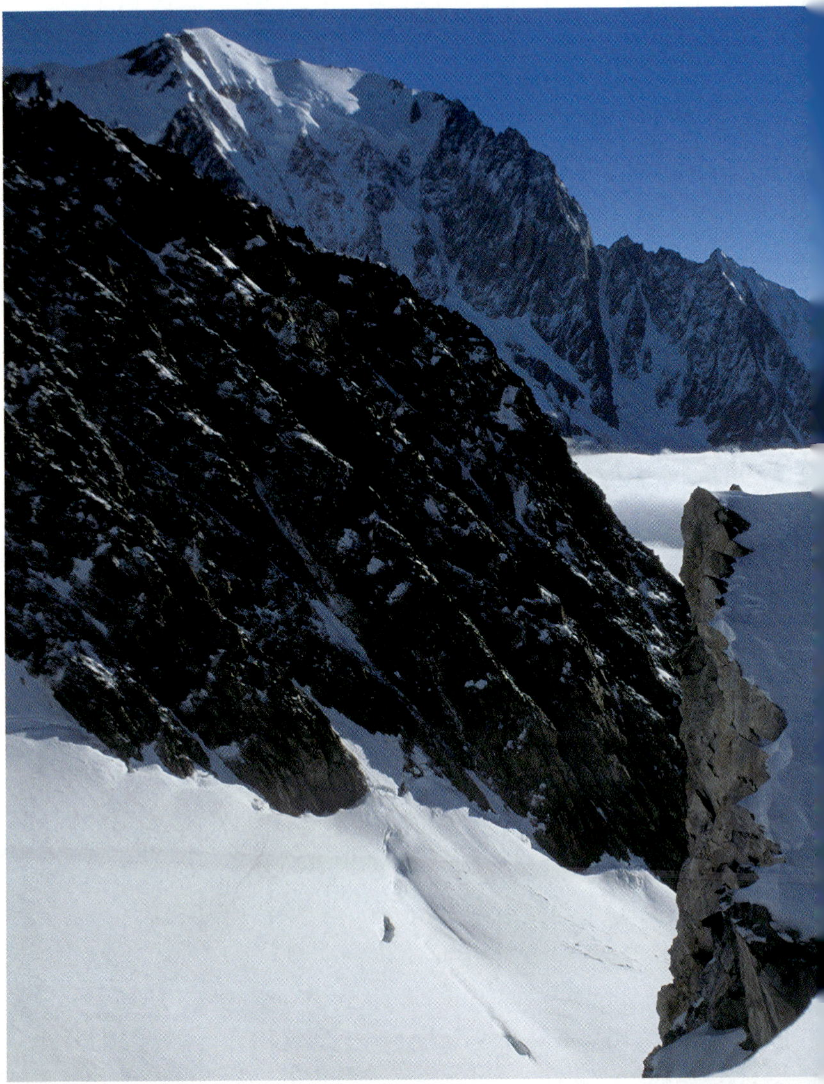

The Miage - Bionnassay Route

The Royal Traverse

The Miage-Bionnassay Route

**The aesthetic, logic and length of the Miage – Bionnassay Route make it one of the great alpine traverses.
It is one of the most enjoyable ways to climb Mont Blanc: a three or four-day journey where the summits meet the skies.**

The route described here may seem to fall outside the criteria that characterise the other "ordinary routes" on Mont Blanc, as it is a physically strenuous and technically demanding high-altitude traverse along knife-edge ridges.
The Miage – Bionnassay combines all the features that mountaineers dream of, making it the perfect route for experienced climbers and an objective to aspire to for others: truly a Royal Traverse.
Not one single aspect of the route is unpleasant or off-putting. Starting from the Contamines Valley, height is gained progressively, the technical difficulties are motivating without being excessive, the route is varied and follows vertiginous ridges up a quiet and unspoilt face of Mont Blanc, and, of course, the views are magnificent.
It is a route to dream of and then share with your guide.
It is a route that reminds you that there is more to mountaineering than reaching the summit.
It is a route that will reveal new horizons!

CHARACTERISTICS OF THE ROUTE

ADVANTAGES
- Long route: three days to get to the summit of Mont Blanc.
- Varied route: walking on glaciers, climbing ridges, snow, ice and rock.
- Technical route: narrow ridges, sections of rock climbing.
- Unspoilt route.
- No ski lifts.
- Committing route.
- A lot of height gain.

DISADVANTAGES
- For some, the advantages can become disadvantages...

A little history

Women on Mont Blanc

"I was a poor servant. One day, the guides said to me: we're going up, come with us. The foreigners want to see you and take you to the top. That made my mind up and I set off with them. At the Grand Plateau, I could go no further. I was very ill and I lay down in the snow. I was gasping for air like an overheated chicken. They took my arms; they pulled me, but at the Rochers Rouges I could go no further, so I said to them: Throw me in a crevasse and go where you like. The guides replied; you have to get to the top. They picked me up, they dragged me, they pushed me and they carried me, and finally we got to the top. When I got to the summit, I couldn't see very well, I couldn't breath or speak. They said I was a pitiful sight."

That was the ninth ascent, on 14th July 1808. Jacques Balmat, his two sons, Ferdinand and Gédéon, Pierre-Marie Frasserand, and Victor and Michel Tairraz, took a woman from Chamonix, called Marie Paradis, with them.

Marie Paradis

Miss Henriette d'Angeville's motives were completely different. Keenly interested in the world around her, she was stubborn in her insistence that she wanted to go. Her family and friends did everything to dissuade her. She reached the summit on 4th September 1838, accompanied by 20 guides. *"And now, Miss"*, said Couttet, *"you have to go higher than Mont Blanc! Joining hands with Desplans, they lifted her above their heads."*

Henriette d'Angeville

Little snow fell in the early part of the winter of 1875-1876. A small group of travellers had stayed in Chamonix and, as the days passed, a spirit of competition grew up amongst them.

On 30th December 1875, Isabella Straton climbed as far as the Grands Mulets.

During the next few days, Miss Brevoort and her nephew Coolidge made three attempts. During the third, they reached the Grand Plateau. On 20th January 1876, the men had a go. The painter Gabriel Loppé and James Eccles also reached the Grand Plateau. A week later, Miss Straton was once again on the mountain. Fog, the lateness of the hour and an accident to a porter prevented them from passing the Bosses. Her fingers froze, so they were rubbed with snow and brandy. Unperturbed, she tried again and at 3 p.m. on 31st January, Miss Straton, together with her usual guide Jean Charlet (whom she would later marry, but that's another wonderful story), Sylvain Couttet and the porter Michel Balmat found themselves at the top of Mont Blanc. It was the first winter ascent. The thermometer showed -24C°.

Turning to the Aiguille de Bionnassay, the key summit in the Royal Traverse, the first ascent was in 1888, by Miss Katherin Richardson with the guides Jean-Baptiste Bich and Émile Rey. From the Col de Miage, and then traversing to the Dôme du Goûter, the lady showed us the way!

Meta Brevoort

Isabella Straton

Katherin Richardson

> "I couldn't wait to celebrate my engagement, to marry him under the most radiant sun and to get drunk on the great and powerful memories that I brought back from that day, from that delicious moment I spent resting at its summit (...) What happiness that it is only my mind that has fallen for such an icy lover!"
>
> **Henriette d'Angeville**
> The "fiancée" of Mont Blanc

The Miage-Bionnassay Route 131

The ascent of Henriette d'Angeville, as depicted by Palisse

Route description

Dômes de Miage — Aiguille de Bionnassay — Mont Blanc

Route tips

The route is climbed in three stages: the approach to the Conscrits hut, the traverse of the Dômes de Miage to the Durier hut, and finally the ascent of the l'Aiguille de Bionnassay, the Dôme du Goûter and Mont Blanc.

If the weather is perfectly stable, with a large anti-cyclone sitting over the Alps, a rest day can be taken at the Durier hut before continuing to the top of Mont Blanc. Once again, we would like to underline how important it is to be properly acclimatised if you want to enjoy the climb to the full and be able to maintain a safe and steady pace throughout. The times given for the Royal Traverse include the descent by the Goûter Route.

GPS			
	Tré-la-Tête hut: 32T E 0323 938 N 5073 400 Conscrits hut: 32T E 0326 300 N 5072 814	Durier hut: 32T E 0329 963 N 5076 925 Piton des Italiens: 32T E 0331 475 N 5078 255	Vallot shelter: 32T E 0333 185 N 5078 418 Mont Blanc: 32T E 0334 118 N 5077 668

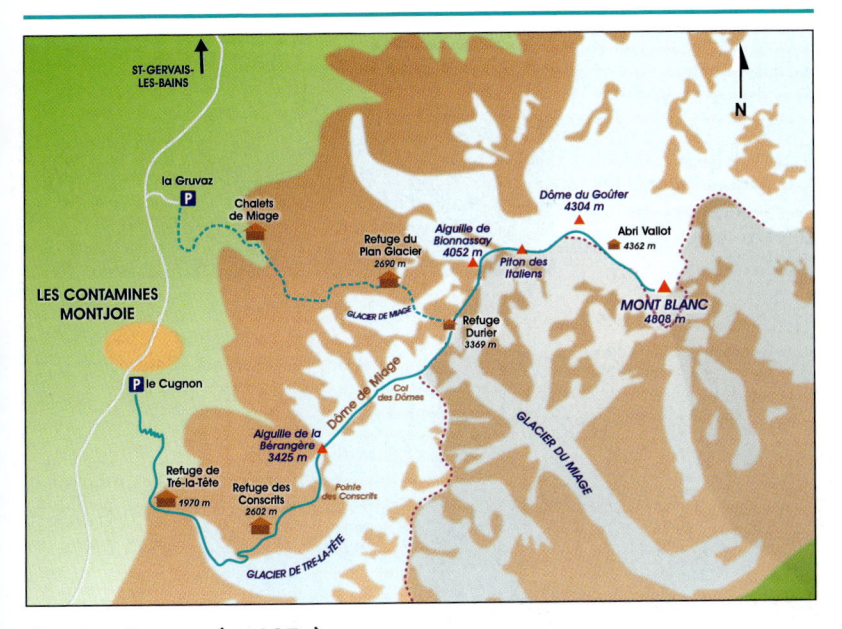

Day 1 = 5 hours (+1427m)
- Le Cugnon car park (1175m) -> Tré-la-Tête hut (1970m) = 2hrs (+795m)
- Tré-la-Tête hut (1970m) -> Conscrits hut (2602m) = 3hrs (+632m)

Day 2 = 7 hours 30 minutes (+1283m/-527m)
- Conscrits hut (2602m) -> Aiguille de la Bérangère (3425m) = 3hrs (+623m)
- Aiguille de la Bérangère (3425m) -> Col de la Bérangère (3348m) = 30mins (-77m)
- Col de la Bérangère (3348m) -> Summit 3670 = 1hr (+322m)
- Summit 3670 -> Col des Dômes (3564m) = 30mins (-50m/+13m/-69m)
- Col des Dômes (3564m) -> Durier hut (3369m) = 2hrs 30mins (+109m/-331m/+29m)

Day 3 = 14 hours 30 minutes (+1593m/-2590m)
- Durier hut (3369m) -> Aiguille de Bionnassay (4040m) = 3hrs 30mins (+671m)
- Aiguille de Bionnassay (4040m) -> Piton des Italiens (4002m) = 1hr 30mins (-152m/+114m)
- Piton des Italiens (4002m) -> Col du Dôme (4255m) = 2hrs (+253m)
- Col du Dôme (4255m) -> Vallot hut (4362m) = 30mins (+107m)
- Vallot hut (4362m) -> Mont Blanc (4808m) = 2hrs (+446m)
- Mont Blanc (4808m) -> Nid d'Aigle (2372m) = 5hrs (-2436m)

From Les Contamines to the Conscrits hut

Start point:
Car park at the hamlet of Le Cugnon (1100m), on the left of the road 1km after Les Contamines.

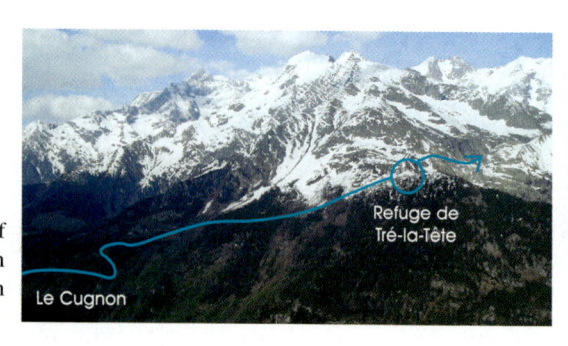

① From the car park, follow the path southwards through the forest. Follow the signs to "Refuge de Tré-la-Tête".

A good path leads to the hut, which lies at the foot of the Grande Roche de Tré-la-Tête (1970m, 2hrs).

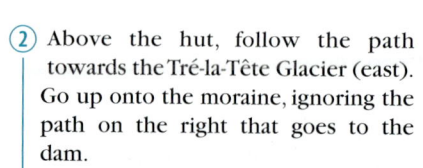

② Above the hut, follow the path towards the Tré-la-Tête Glacier (east). Go up onto the moraine, ignoring the path on the right that goes to the dam.

After a few hairpin bends, contour round to cross the "Mauvais Pas", and then descend onto the glacier at the flat area under Tré-la-Petite (1hr).

③ The glacier is partly covered by rocks. Follow the track, at first staying close to the moraine to avoid the crevasses, and then moving into the centre of the glacier (cairns). Go past the first break of slope to reach a flatter section at Tré-la-Grande (30mins).

✓ Tré-la-Tête supposedly got its name because it has three distinct heads: the northern summit or Aiguille Blanche (3892m), the Aiguille Centrale (3930m) and the Aiguille Occidentale (3895m).

④ At around 2225m, leave the centre of the glacier and come back towards the left (the true right bank) via a small plateau at the foot of the seracs that mark a major change in the slope and direction of the glacier (crampons often necessary).

⑤ From here, you have to get to a large diagonal gully that is hidden behind a rock spur (blue arrows painted on the rocks). This gully takes you to the top of the first line of cliffs below the Pointe de Tré-la-Grande.

⑥ At around 2270m, start climbing the above-mentioned diagonal gully. The route crosses very unstable ground (helmet advisable). A short hand-line (left bank of the gully) has been put in place to make a tricky section safer. Towards the top of the gully, the route bears left across some rocky slabs equipped with fixed ropes. The path, which is regained at around 2325m by contouring round to the left of a steep cliff, leads to a sort of plateau at 2375m (1hr).

⑦ The path then traverses eastwards between small cliffs and ravines to get to the Conscrits hut (2602m, 30mins).
3 hours from the Tré-la-Tête hut, 5 hours from Les Contamines.

The Miage-Bionnassay Route 137

From the Conscrits hut to the Durier hut via the Dômes de Miage

The traverse described here goes from the Conscrits hut to the Aiguille de la Bérangère, and then traverses the five Dômes de Miage (3670m, 3666m, 3633m, 3673m, 3672m) before descending to the Col de Miage and the Durier hut.

The line of the Dômes de Miage forms a beautiful, three kilometre-long ridge that is sometimes known as "Mont Blanc de Saint Gervais". This ridge is not technically difficult, but some sections can be a little delicate when snow conditions are not optimum. In contrast, the descent to the Col de Miage requires a certain amount of route finding ability and involves down-climbing over rock and mixed ground.

⑧ From above the Conscrits hut, go onto the crest of the moraine, from where the summit of the Aiguille de la Bérangère can be seen (to be reconnoitred the day before while it is light). Climb northwards and cross the upper snowfields of Tré-la-Grande. Follow snow slopes towards the Pointe des Conscrits (cairns). These slopes lead to a dip just to the left of the Pointe. Climb the ridge on the left to reach the easy-angled snow slopes that lead to the summit of the Aiguille de la Bérangère (3425m) (3hrs).

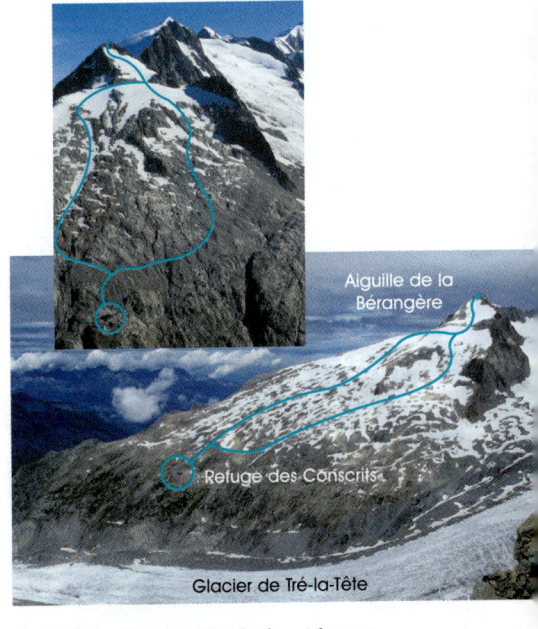

⑨ From the summit of the Bérangère, descend to the Col de la Bérangère (3348m), first via a narrow, rocky ridge, and then by a frequently corniced snow ridge (30mins). From the Col, follow the ridge towards the south-west. This is the ordinary route for the first Dôme (Summit 3670m). It is possible to climb the easy but broken rocks on the right, or the snow slopes on the left (1hr).

Dôme 3670

Mont Blanc

Dôme 3666

Dôme 3633

Col 3620

⑩ Follow an almost horizontal ridge (easy) to Summit 3666m.

⑪ Go down to a snowy saddle (3620m) (escape is possible down the snow slopes that lead to the Tré-la-Tête Glacier), and then back up to Summit 3633m. The ridge is often corniced.

The Miage-Bionnassay Route **139**

⑫ Continue along the ridge to the Col des Dômes (3564m) (30mins from Summit 3670m, 2hrs from the Aiguille de la Bérangère).

It is possible to descend from the Col des Dômes to the Conscrits hut by the Tré-la-Tête Glacier.

Dôme 3673

Col des Dômes

⑬ From the Col des Dômes, climb easily up to Summit 3673m (the highest point of the Dômes de Miage).

Dôme 3670 3666
3633

Glacier de Tré-la-Tête

Col des Dômes

140 The Miage-Bionnassay Route

⑭ From Summit 3673m, the route follows the line of the ridge, sometimes on rock, sometimes on snow, depending on the conditions.

⑮ From Summit 3673m, traverse to Summit 3672m.

✓ The ridge traverse from the Dômes de Miage to the Durier hut is not technically difficult, but the slopes on either side of the ridge are very steep. On the Italian side, these slopes are warmed by the sun, on the French side they are dark and forbidding. This is another reminder that there is a big difference between exposure and difficulty. The party must continuously adapt its rope work to the vagaries of the terrain and the quantity and quality of the snow.

⑯ Continue to a subsidiary summit (3665m) and start a more marked descent.

The Miage-Bionnassay Route **141**

⑰ Descend a snow slope on the right to reach the foot of a small twin-peaked summit, which will be avoided on the right. This is the point where the ridge curves round from a north-easterly direction to a north-north-easterly direction.

Aiguille de Bionnassay

Mont Blanc

Refuge Durier

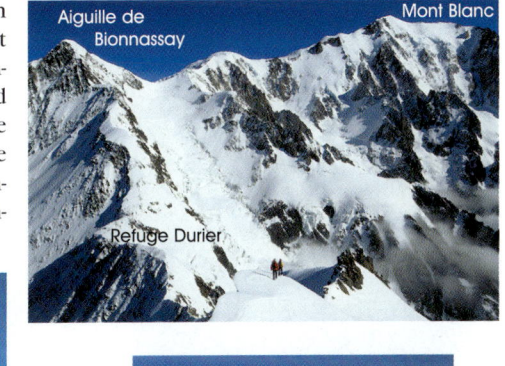

⑱ Contour round the Italian side of the twin-peaked summit.

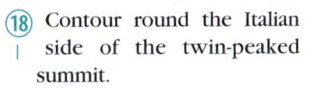

⑲ Come back onto the ridge and go down a steep slope, staying slightly on the French side of the ridge (red dots). This can be quite delicate, but if necessary the slope can be descended by a 20-metre abseil. Once at the foot of this slope, go back onto the crest of the ridge.

142 The Miage-Bionnassay Route

Aiguille de Bionnassay

Refuge Durier

⑳ Go along the ridge, staying slightly on the Italian side (delicate).

㉑ Go past a small saddle (3345m), and then over a small rise (3390m).
Go past the Col de Miage (3358m), and then go up a short distance to the Durier hut (3369m, 2hrs from Summit 3673m, 7hrs 30mins from the Conscrits hut).

✓ The Durier hut is a small building anchored to the Col de Miage, at the foot of the Aiguille de Bionnassay. The view from here is exceptional and the sunsets magnificent. The toilets are suspended in mid-air above the French face, and climbers often stayed roped up to use them in case they are blown over by a gust of wind!

From the Durier hut to the Aiguille de Bionnassay

㉒ The general line of the route follows the south-south-west ridge of the Bionnassay.

㉓ Climb above the Durier hut to go around a small cliff. Go up the snow slope, or follow the track up the scree (cairns).
Where the slope eases at around 3600m (45mins), stay on the French side of the ridge to avoid the cornices that overhang the Italian side.

㉔ Go up the slope to a first summit. A ridge of snow and rock (3700m) leads to a second rocky summit.

㉕ Traverse the French side of a snowy ridge (cornices on the Italian side) to a small col (3780m) at the foot of the large step that is the key to climbing the Aiguille de Bionnassay (2hrs from the Durier hut). Go along a series of snowy ledges to get to a good, rock terrace on the south-east side of the ridge.

Aiguille de Bionnassay

Col 3780

㉖ Climb a small corner (grade III) that is capped by a jammed block. Move right, and then follow a ledge slightly leftwards towards the crest of the ridge.

A good terrace provides a belay. Climb two parallel flakes (III+) up to a terrace (crampon marks). Traverse behind a flake on the French side (also possible on the Italian side), and then follow a line of good flake holds, near the crest of the ridge, on the French side.

Move back right into the corner and follow a corner-chimney to the top of the step. The exit is blocked by a small flake. There is an abseil point at the top of the corner.

The Miage-Bionnassay Route | **145**

㉗ Above the good terraces, there is a final rock-step that can be avoided on the right by a tongue of snow. This step leads to the top of the Bionnassay rocks (3930m, 1hr).

✓ The Bionnassay rock step is not very difficult (grade 3/4 on a scale of 9), but it is true rock-climbing and not just scrambling. In good conditions (dry rock, not too cold, no wind) these two pitches are good fun. However, if the rock is wet or partially covered in snow and ice, or if you are being buffeted by the wind, or if your fingers are numb with cold... the rock can feel very steep and the drop very intimidating! With the right gear, you will be much safer and feel much more comfortable. The leader should carry a rack of nuts and a few extra slings for runners and fix belays.

㉘ A snowy ridge leads from the top of the rocky summit to the Aiguille de Bionnassay. 3hrs 30mins from the Durier hut.

From the Aiguille de Bionnassay to Mont Blanc

㉙ The ridge between the Aiguille de Bionnassay and Mont Blanc is one of the narrowest in the massif. It can be both difficult and dangerous if the snow is unstable or if it is covered in ice. Some sections are extremely intimidating and leave most climbers with very vivid memories.

㉚ From the summit, follow the Italian side of the ridge eastwards (easy) down to a small col.

㉛ Contour round the large, characteristic cornice on the right.

The Miage-Bionnassay Route **147**

㉜ Go back onto the narrow ridge that leads to a small rocky spur. Go down to the Col de Bionnassay, at first staying on the crest of the ridge and then moving onto the Italian side to avoid the cornices that form on the French side.
Move back onto the crest to reach the Col de Bionnassay (3888m, 1hr from the Aiguille).

Dôme du Goûter
Piton des Italiens
Col de Bionnassay

㉝ Climb the Piton des Italiens (4002m, 30mins), staying on the Italian side. From the Piton des Italiens, go down towards a col and then go over a rise and a snowy saddle to reach the ridge that leads to the Dôme du Goûter.

☞ **Detailed description as for the Pope Route p.11**

㉞ Go around the left (south) side of the Dôme to reach the Col du Dôme (2hrs), the Bosses Ridge and the summit of Mont Blanc.

☞ **Detailed description as for the Goûter Route p.53**

148 The Miage-Bionnassay Route

"The day was breaking. One more day... Luckily the weather was fine. That was the answer to all our questions; time for joy and action when, in spite of a gnawing pain and crushing weariness, everything becomes suddenly shot with wonderful certainty. Hail to thee, O world of adventure!"

Georges Sonnier
Terre du Ciel - 1959

AN ALTERNATIVE ROUTE TO THE DURIER HUT BY THE PLAN GLACIER HUT

The Durier hut can be reached directly from the hamlet of Gruvaz, via the Plan Glacier hut. In this way, the Bionnassay - Mont Blanc Traverse can be done in two days.
If necessary, it is also possible to descend directly from the Durier hut to the valley, without going back towards the Dômes de Miage (description p.153).
Similarly, it is possible to descend into Italy, via the steep slopes above the Bionnassay Italien Glacier and the Miage Glacier.

There is also a longer version of this approach, starting from the village of Bionnassay (car park at the hamlet of Le Crozat (1420m), just after Bionnassay).
From here, the route goes over the Col de Tricot (2120m, 2hrs), and then follows a path across the lower slopes of the Arête de Tricot to reach the moraine and the Plan Glacier hut (2680m, 2hrs, 4hrs from Le Crozat). This path crosses very steep ground and requires a sure foot, despite the presence of cables to help walkers over the more difficult sections. Even with these cables, this route is only feasible in the summer after all the snow has melted and during periods of dry weather.
A final option is to reach the Col de Tricot from the Col de Bellevue (reached from the TMB or the Bellevue cable car - see Goûter chapter, p.48). This last option may be long, but it has the advantage of allowing you to leave your car at the arrival point of the descent. From Bellevue, follow the variant of the Tour du Mont-Blanc. Just before the Chalet de l'Are, descend rightwards to pick up the path to the large footbridge across the Bionnassay. Go up to the Chalets de Tricot (ruins) and through the Combe de Tricot to reach the Col du Tricot (2120m, 2hrs).

150 The Miage-Bionnassay Route

① a From Saint-Gervais, follow the road to Les Contamines, continuing along it to the car park at La Gruvaz (1150m). Go across the bridge and follow the 4-wheel drive track up to the Chalets de Miage (1559m, 1hr on foot). In the summer, you can eat and/or sleep here. There is restricted access for 4-wheel drive vehicles, but it is possible to hire a 4-wheel drive taxi in Saint-Gervais.

From the Chalets de Miage, go up through the Pâturages de Miage. The path goes up a small cliff (red marks) to the right of a waterfall, and then climbs an increasingly distinct moraine. At around 2500m, the route traverses rightwards to get to the base of the large moraine on the right bank of the Miage Glacier.

② a Go up the moraine as far as the cliff that shelters the Plan Glacier hut (2680m, 2hrs 30mins, 3hrs 30mins from La Gruvaz).

③ a The route from the Plan Glacier hut follows a path along a series of rocky ledges to a flattish area on the Miage Glacier, at around 2800 m. A gully leads from the other side of the glacier to a point just above the Col de Miage.

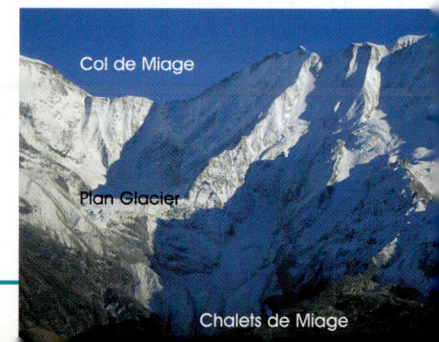

④ ᵃ So, from the hut, descend slightly to go round the toilets (!) and follow the track that goes up across the cliff (red dots). Go up a small cliff with the help of a cable (2740m). A rightwards, ascending traverse takes you to a second set of cables (2775m) which lead up to a small ridge (2810m).

⑤ ᵃ Traverse rightwards across a scree slope and a snowfield, and then go up a second small cliff to a ridge (2850m). A cable has been placed along this ridge.

⑥ ᵃ At the end of the cable, descend slightly along the ridge (cairns), and then head leftwards along a sort of ledge. This south-facing slope has been fitted with cables to facilitate the descent and traverse onto the Miage Glacier (at about 2840m). The first part of the descent is steep, and then it follows sloping slabs directly above the bergschrund. It is recommended to rope people down this section if there is any doubt about their ability to descend safely.

⑦ a Easily cross the flat part of the glacier (crevasses) to reach the left bank at about 2880m: the red dots along the ledge will guide you to the rocky slopes in the wall that descends from the Col de Miage.

⑧ a The route works its way up through occasional areas of loose rock or snow (the top of the climb zigzags through large blocks). If the snow conditions are good, the obvious, large gully on the left of the face can be climbed. It comes out slightly above the col and the bivouac. 2hrs 30mins from Plan Glacier, 5hrs from La Gruvaz.

Escape from the Durier hut to the Plan Glacier hut

(9) a The descent starts down a steep slope, made up of large, unstable blocks, to the left of the toilets. Avoid the areas threatened by stone fall from the secondary gullies that criss-cross the face, as best you can. The route finding is much easier in the bottom third of the face.

When you get above the glacier, head right to find a ledge dotted with red paint marks. (When snow conditions are good, the gullies on the right, as shown here in the photograph, or on the left, provide fast descents, as long as you are at ease on steep slopes).

Go onto the glacier (2880m) and traverse across it on a sort of small plateau (2810m).

Go over to the right bank of the Miage Glacier (bergschrund) and use the cables to climb the slabs of rock. Follow a ledge leftwards, and then go up the ridge for a short distance (cairns). A cable enables you to traverse left and go over the two crests.

Go across a snowfield and a scree slope to get to the cables that lead down the final cliff to the Plan Glacier hut (2hrs).

Descent from Mont Blanc to the Durier hut

(35) From Mont Blanc, descend the Bosses Ridge (detailed description as for the Goûter Route, p.57) to the Col du Dôme. Bear left to leave the track down to the Goûter hut and go between the summit of the Dôme du Goûter (which will be just on your right) and the precipices that plunge down to the Dôme Glacier on the Italian side.

(36) South-west of the Dôme, the slope turns into a ridge that becomes quite narrow as it reaches the Piton des Italiens.

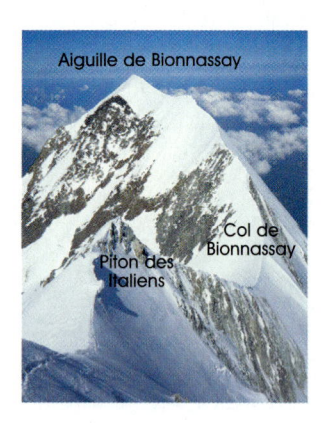

(37) Go past the Piton des Italiens (4002m, slight ascent), and then descend easily to the Col de Bionnassay (3888m).
Follow the ridge up to the subsidiary summit of the Bionnassay, staying on the Italian side of the ridge to avoid the cornices on the French side.

The Miage-Bionnassay Route 155

38) Go along the narrow, horizontal ridge, and then up to the large cornice. Contour round the Italian side of this cornice and go easily up to the summit of the Bionnassay (4052m).

39) Head due south down the snow slope, going leftwards around a subsidiary summit, to reach wide ledges above a cliff. Abseil down the cliff (abseil point in-situ) to reach more ledges, which are often covered in snow.
Follow a band of snow down to a small col (3780m).
Follow the ridge over a subsidiary summit, and then, still on the French side, go down to the base of the widening ridge (3600m).

40) Follow the scree slope (track and cairns) or the snowfield to the Durier hut.

156 The Miage-Bionnassay Route

From the Durier hut to the Conscrits hut via the Dômes de Miage

(41) Descend to the Col de Miage, and then go over a rise (3390m). Continue along the Italian side of the ridge to get to a steep step that is climbed on the French side (red marks). Go back onto the crest of the ridge, and then up to the twin-peaked summit. Go round the Italian side of this summit, and then follow a snow slope to the shoulder on the ridge. From here, go up to a subsidiary summit at 3665m.

(42) Stay on the crest of the ridge to reach the point 3580m (from here it is possible to get to the Col Infranchissable and descend easily to the Tré-la-Tête Glacier).

㊸ To traverse the Dômes de Miage, "simply" follow the crest of the ridge over the Dômes. Successively go over Summits 3672m, 3673m (highest points of the Dômes) to reach the Col des Dômes (3564m), and then go up to Summit 3633m. Traverse Dôme 3666m to Dôme 3670m.

㊹ From the last Dôme, descend to the Col de la Bérangère (3348m), from where it is possible to go down onto the Tré-la-Tête Glacier.

㊺ Follow a snow slope, and then a rocky slope to reach the Aiguille de la Bérangère (3425m).
Descend the snow slopes to the south, staying to the right of the Pointe des Conscrits.
Finally, descend the snowfields of Tré-la-Grande back to the Conscrits hut.

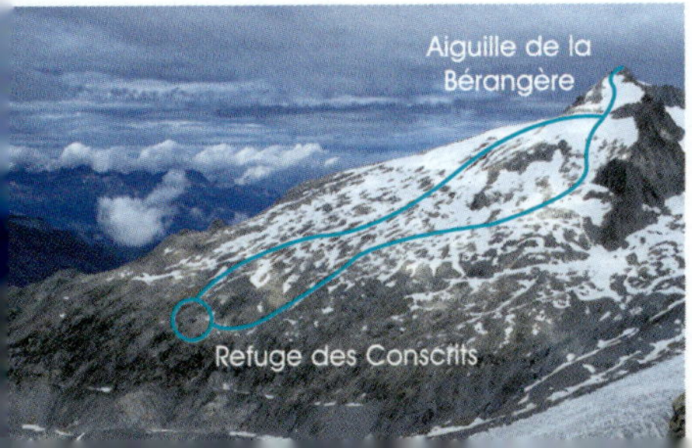

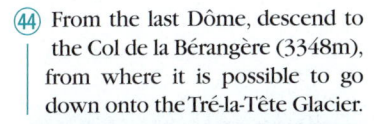

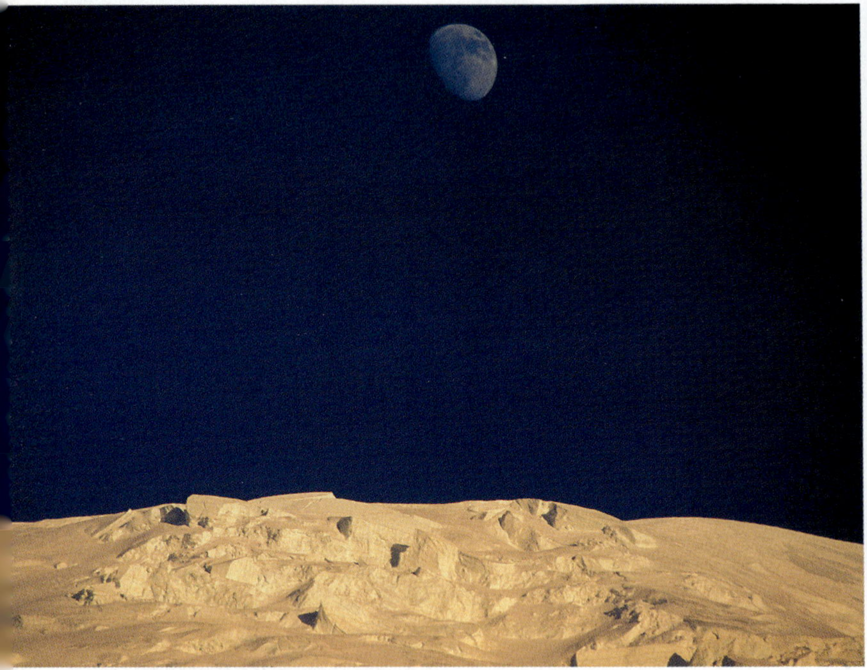

Bibliography

Au royaume du Mont-Blanc. Paul Payot, 1950. La Fontaine de Siloé, 1996.
Ascensions au pays du Mont-Blanc. Jean-Louis Laroche and Florence Lelong. Glénat, 2000.
Chronologie d'une carotte de glace de 20 m au col du Dôme. J. Jouzel, M. Legrand, F. Pinglot, M. Pourchet, L. Reynaud. La Houille Blanche n° 6/7-1984.
Dans le secret des glaciers du Mont-Blanc. Luc Moreau, Robert Vivian. Glénat, 2000.
Dictionnaire de la montagne. Sylvain Jouty and Hubert Odier. Arthaud, 1999.
1786, Chamonix et la conquête du Mont-Blanc. Thérèse Robache. Édimontagne, 1986.
Exploits au Mont Blanc. André Roch. Nuova Edizioni Trelingue, 1987.
Et la montagne conquit l'homme. Myrtil Schwartz. Librairie Fischbacher, 1931.
Études sur les mouvements des neiges au sommet du Mont Blanc. Joseph Vallot.
Guide des livres sur la montagne et l'alpinisme. Jacques Perret. Editions de Belledonne, 1997.
Guide Vallot. Lucien Devies and Pierre Henry. Arthaud, 1978.
Histoire du Mont Blanc. Stephen d'Arve, 1878. La Fontaine de Siloé, 1993.
L'Ascension du Mont-Blanc est affaire d'alpinistes. La Chamoniarde, 2002.
Mont Blanc, conquête de l'Imaginaire. La Fontaine de Siloé.
Le Mont Blanc. Charles Durier, 1923. La Fontaine de Siloé, 2000.
Le Mont Blanc. Stefano Ardito. Gründ.
Le Mont Blanc, vu par les écrivains et les alpinistes. Claire-Eliane Engel. Éditions d'histoire et d'art, 1965.
Mont Blanc et Aiguilles Rouges. Anselme Baud. Nevicata. 2002.
Le Mont Blanc. Routes classiques et voies nouvelles. Claire-Eliane Engel. Victor Attinger, 1946.
Les Alpinistes célèbres. Mazenot, 1957.
Les noms de lieux de la région du Mont-Blanc. Roland Boyer, 1987.
Les Papes du XXe siècle. Yves Marchasson. Ed Desclée.
Le Roman de la montagne. Max Chamson. Christian de Bartillat Editeur. 1987.
Mont-Blanc, ski de randonnée. Éric Delapierre - Franck Gentilini. Vamos, 2000.
Mussolini et l'Italie fasciste. Marco Palla. Casterman - Giunti.
Rapport sur les travaux de sondage exécutés au Mont Blanc. Annales de l'Observatoire du Mont-Blanc de Joseph Vallot.
Sommets du Mont Blanc. Jean-Louis Laroche and Florence Lelong. Glénat, 1996.
Magazines: *Alpes Magazine - Alpirando - La Montagne et Alpinisme - Montagnes Magazine - Vertical*

Contents

Foreword	5
How to use this guide	7
Altitude 4808	
Climbing Mont Blanc is true mountaineering!	10
Is Mont Blanc over-crowded?	11
Reasons for taking a guide	12
Where to find a guide?	12
When to climb Mont Blanc	13
Weather	14
Preparation and medical advice	18
Glaciology	22
Gear	24
Huts	25
A word from the Haute-Savoie PGHM	28
Useful addresses	29
Route descriptions, route finding and GPS	30
The five routes map	32
Mont Blanc in 10 dates	34
The Goûter Route	40
The Three Monts Route	62
The Grands Mulets Route	82
The Pope Route	106
The Miage-Bionnassay Route	126
Bibliography	159

Graphic design and realization: F. Rouxel
Illustrations: EB Créations
Computer graphics: M. Riihimaki et Imag'il
Translation: P. Henderson
Printing: Mâcon Imprimerie - France - 2004
JMEditions - 93 chemin du vieux guide - F-74400 Chamonix
jmeditions@wanadoo.fr
Publication date: June 2004 - ©: 2004 - JMEditions